Discovering Patterns in Mandalas

Beginning Mandalas to Color

by Cynthia Taylor

Exploring Patterns Coloring Books

ISBN-13: 978-0692521991

ISBN-10: 0692521992

Discovering Mandalas

As you picked up this book, you might have asked yourself, *What is a mandala and why would I want to make one?* The mandala (pronounced muhn'-dl-uh) is one of the oldest art forms developed by humans. The word *mandala* is from the ancient language of Sanskrit and means "circle." However, a mandala is much more than just a circle. It is a symbol that represents wholeness, a diagram that illustrates our life in relation to the infinite and divine.

A mandala has a central focal point, and a symmetrical design radiates outward from that center. When you look at a mandala, your eye is drawn toward the center of the geometric or thematic pattern. The center can represent the inner self as well as the center of the universe. A mandala is a picture that tells a story of a journey. As we follow the path through the mandala to the center, we are looking for the wholeness that lies at our own center.

A mandala can describe what we can see as well as things we cannot see — the sun, moon, and earth as well as our feelings and relationships. Exploring the mandala helps us focus our attention and may even help us change how we see ourselves, other people, our planet, and our relation to the divine.

Mandalas have been incorporated into various religious traditions and cultures throughout the ages, from the Indian Buddhist and Hindu to the Tibetan to the Christian to the Aztec and Navajo Indians. Detailed mandalas made of colored sand are still created by modern Tibetan monks and Navajos, requiring many days to complete one pattern. Labyrinths are another kind of mandala found in many cultures. The labyrinth in Chartres Cathedral in France is an example of a mandala in the Christian tradition. The stained glass Gothic rose windows of cathedrals are also mandalas. Even a kaleidoscope design is a type of mandala.

Psychoanalyst Carl Jung believed that the mandala represented a person's unconscious self. Jung believed that creating mandalas helped patients make the unconscious conscious, and both he and his patients created mandalas as a means to personal growth and wholeness.

Coloring a mandala is a creative way to relax after a long, stressful day. It can be a treat you give yourself. It can be a form of meditation. Creating a mandala is a way to express yourself. Let your imagination flow freely as you choose the color combinations you want to use. Perhaps you want to create one mandala in earth tones of brown, yellow, and orange; another in jewel tones of purple, green, red, blue, and magenta; and still another in soft pastels. You can make each row of a pattern one color or alternate colors within the segments on a row to create very different visual effects. You can use crayons, markers, colored pencils, or even gel pens. Each method will give you a different look. If you want a bold look, you might choose markers, whereas colored pencils will allow you to blend and shade color. The more intricate the design, the sharper the tip you will need to use and the steadier your hand will need to be.

Most of all, creating mandalas is fun, so enjoy yourself as you explore their patterns through coloring.

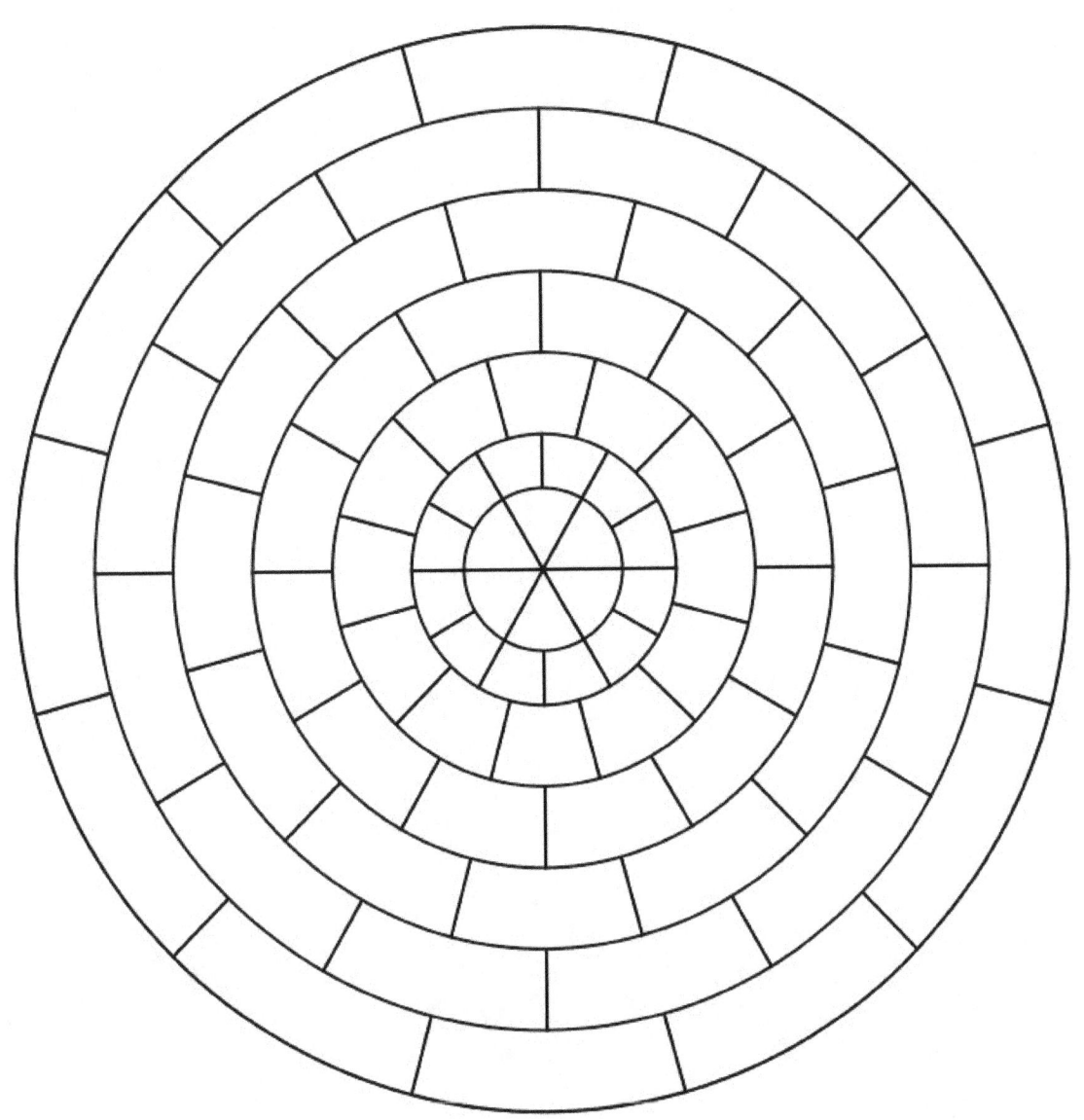

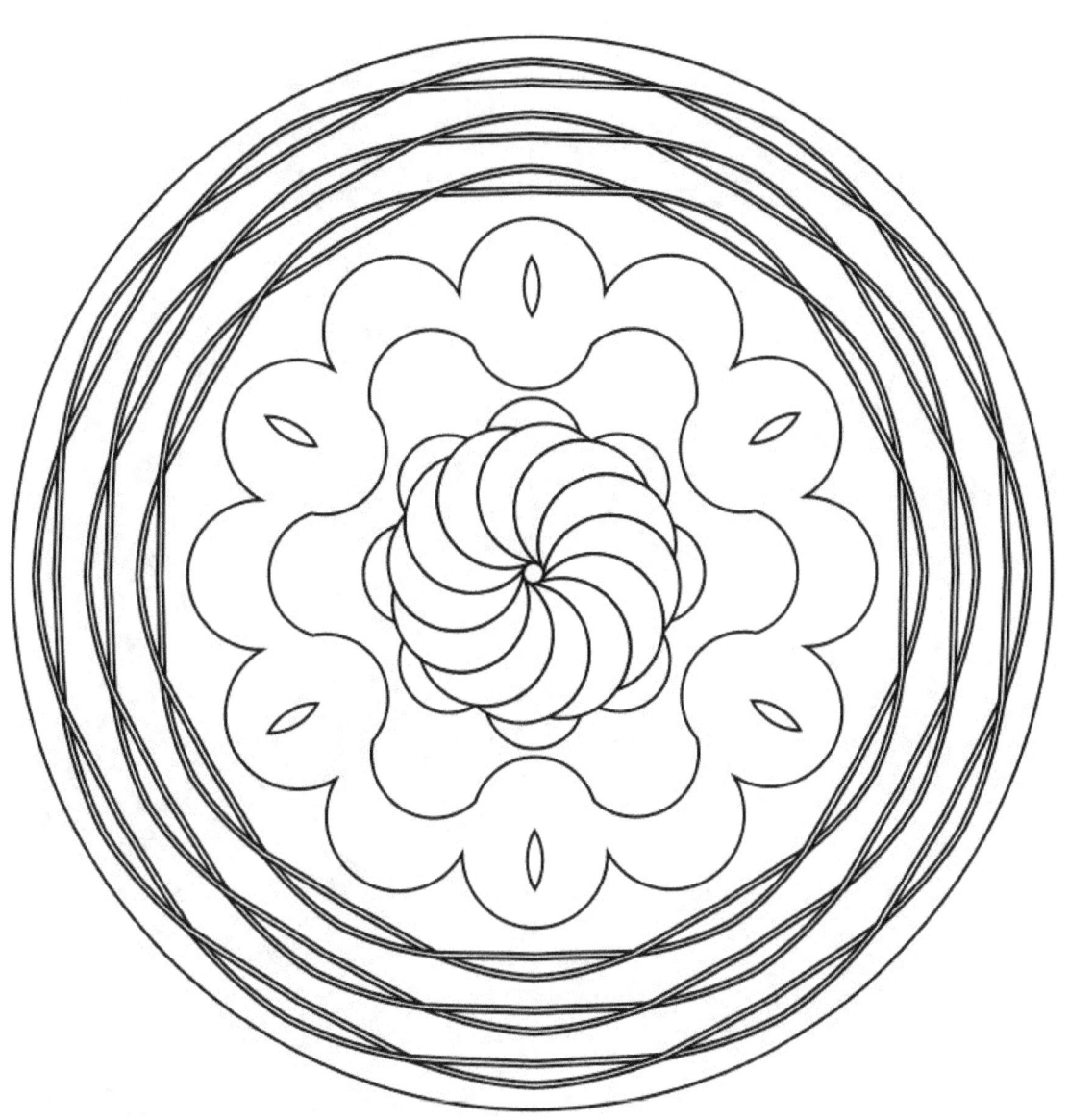

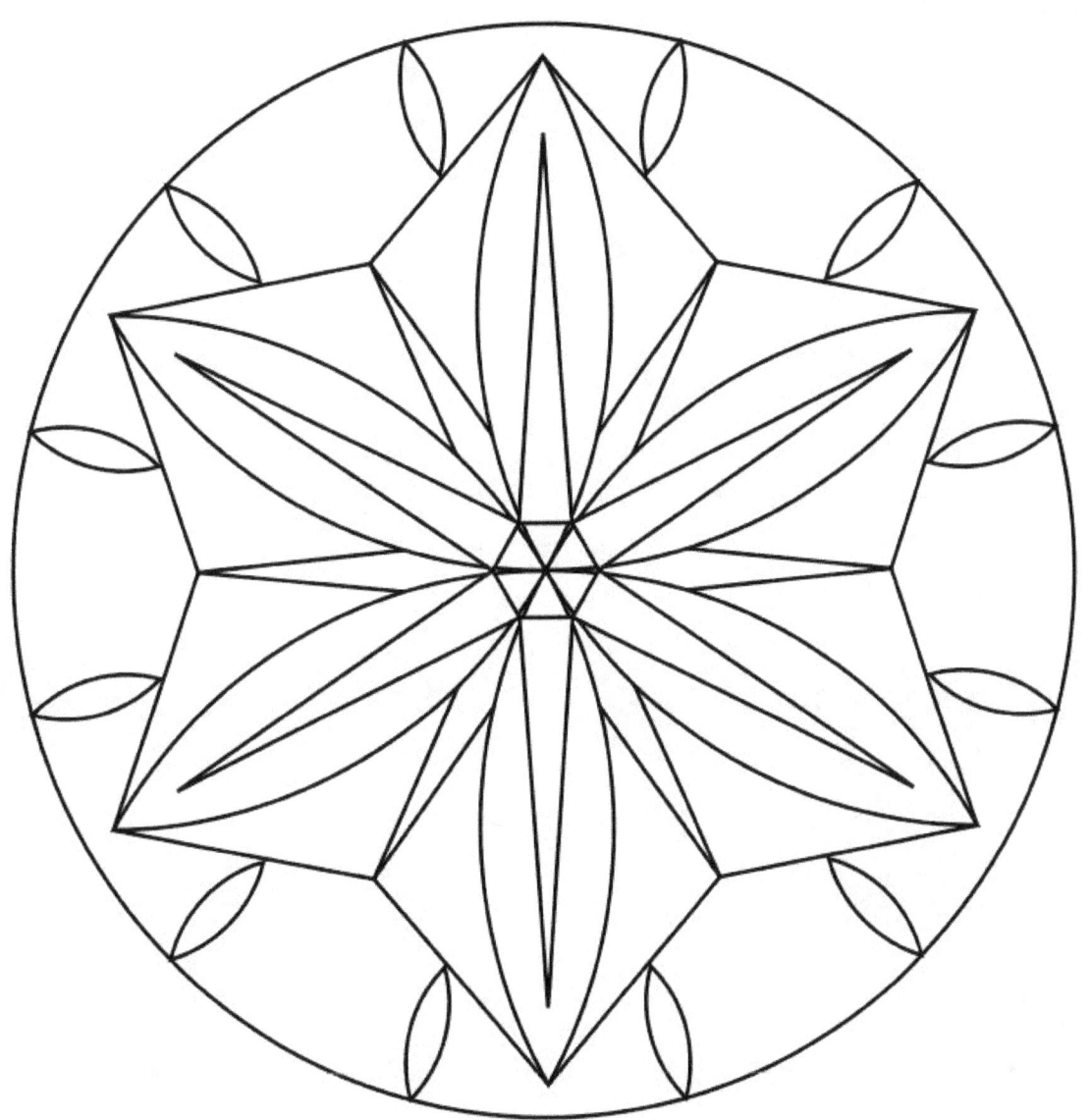

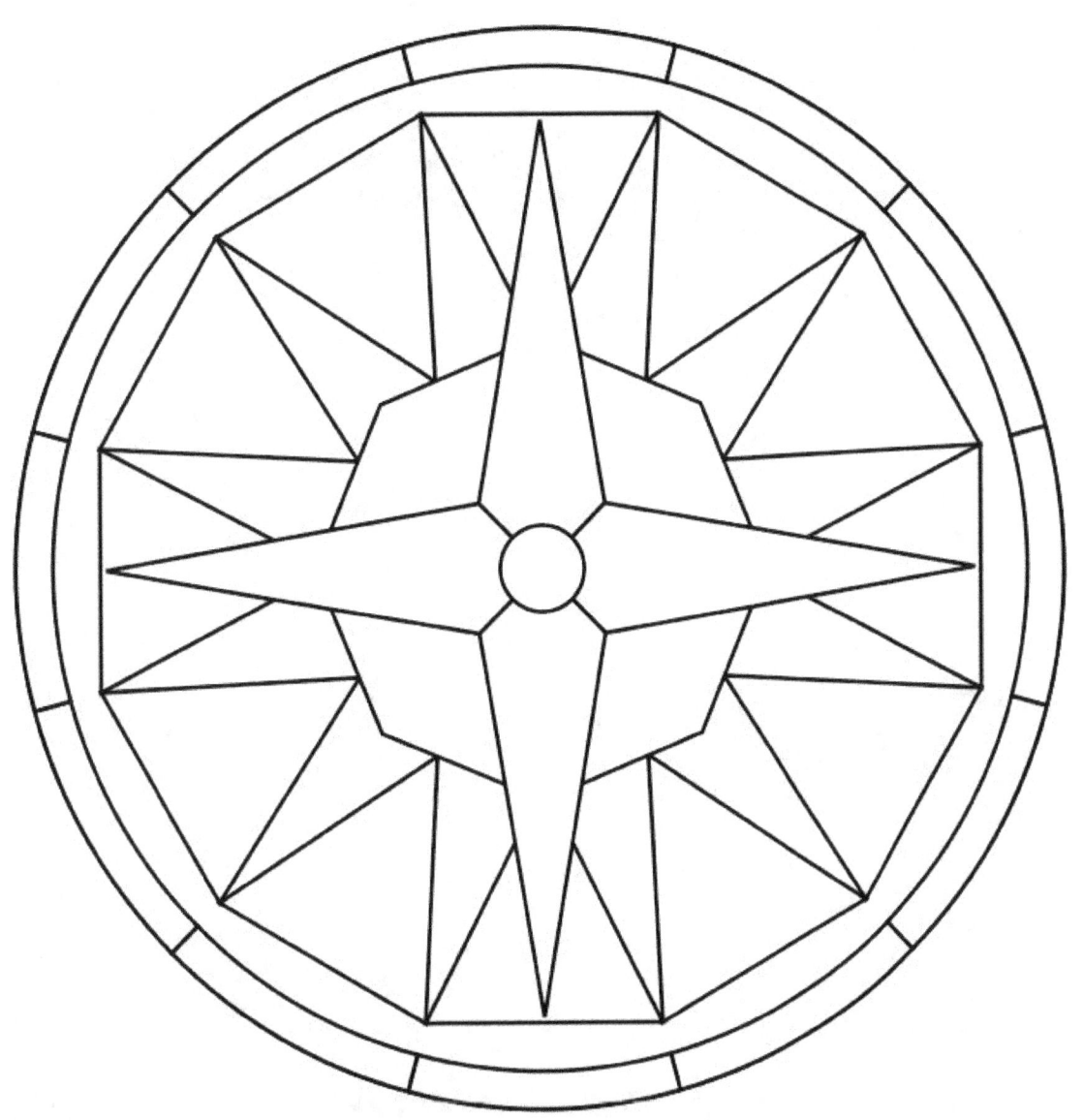

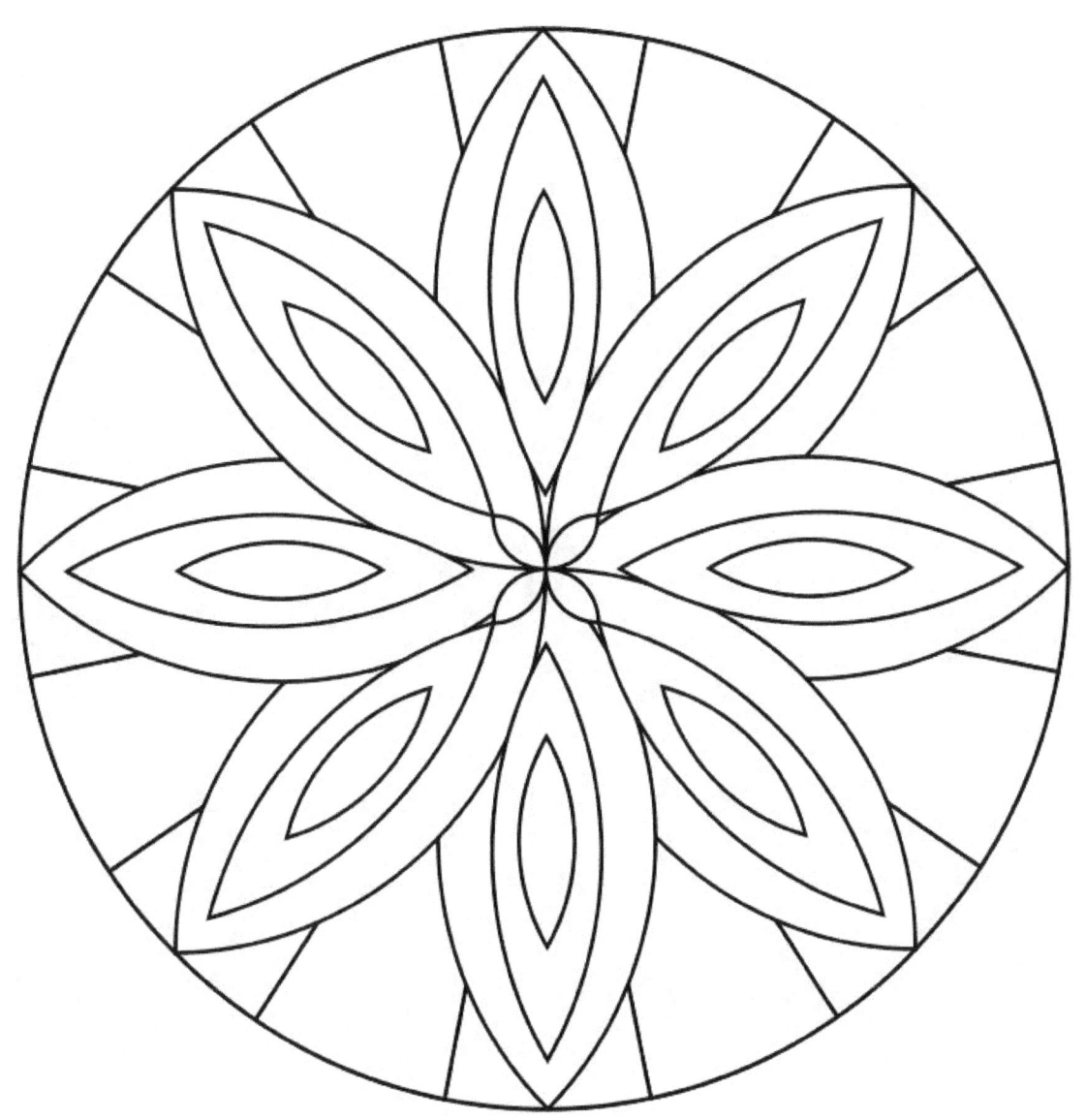

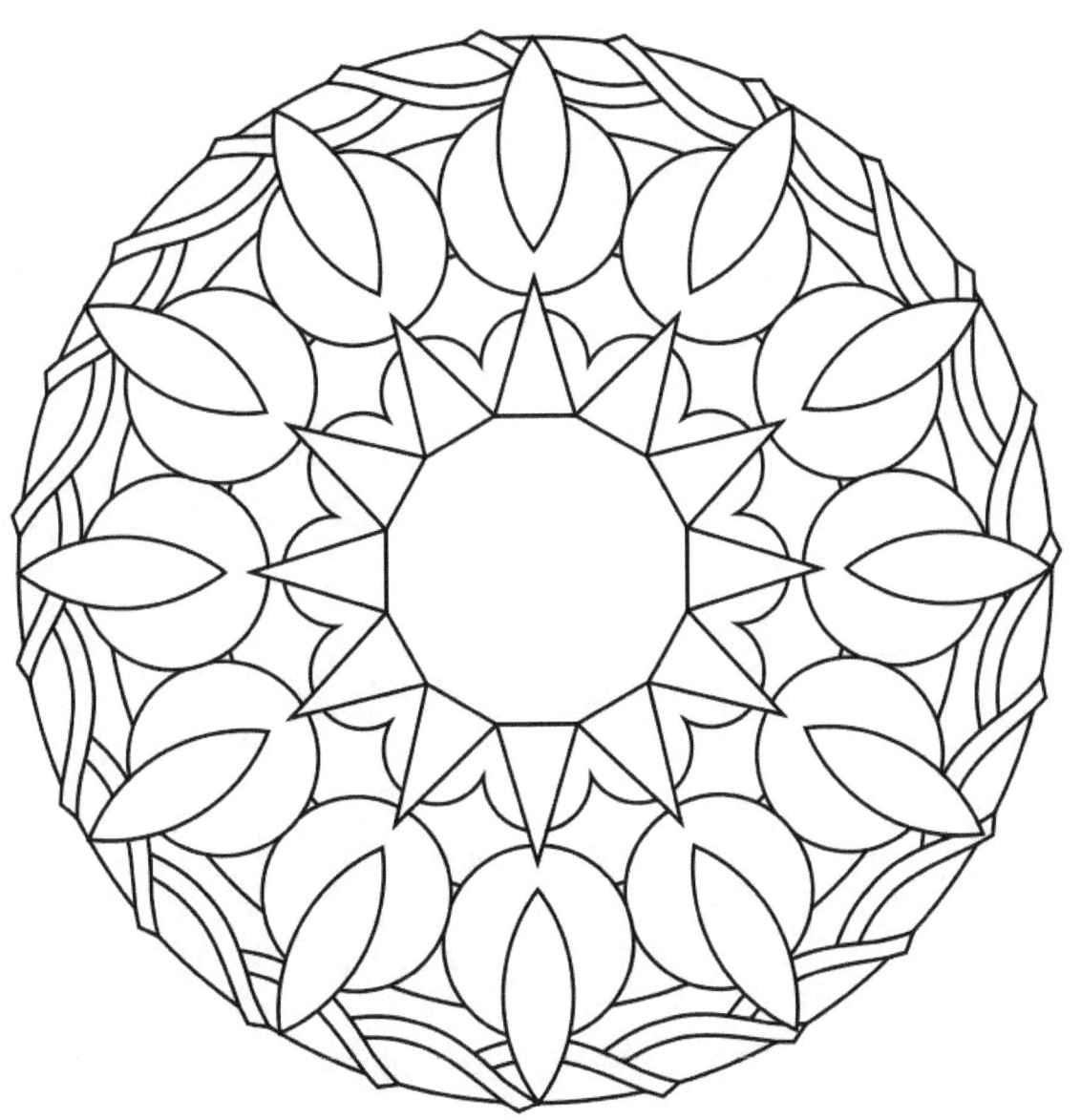

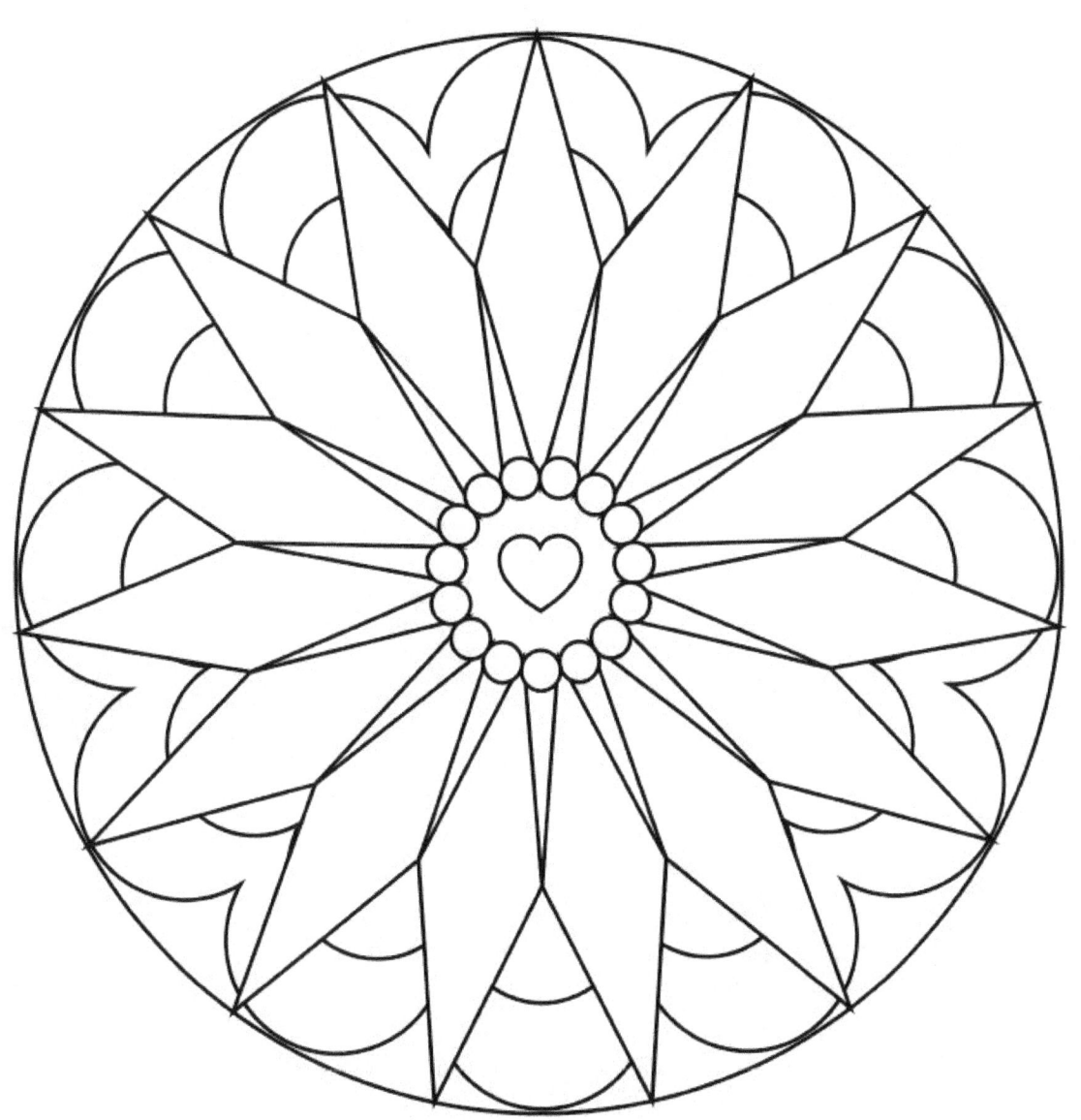

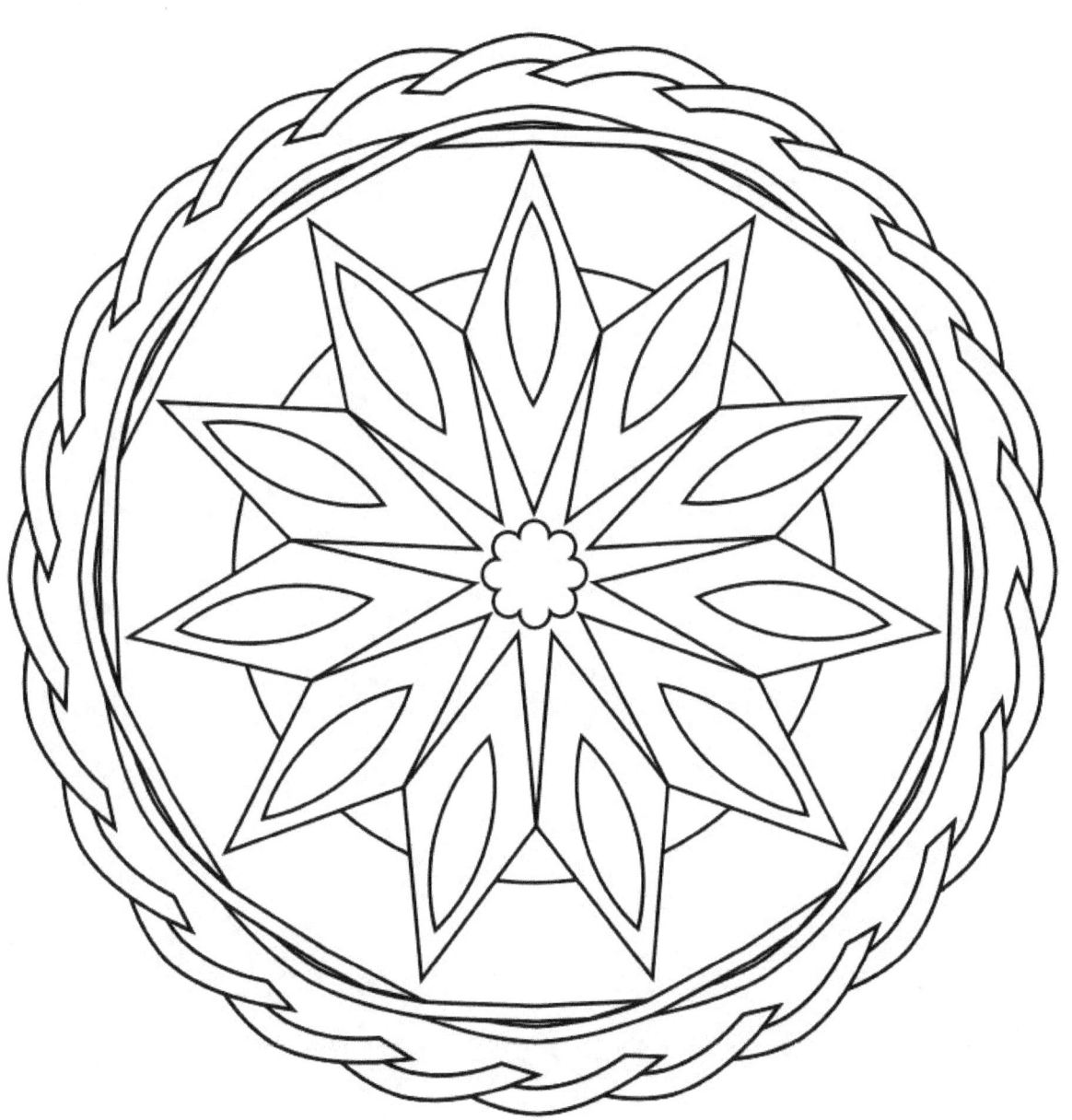

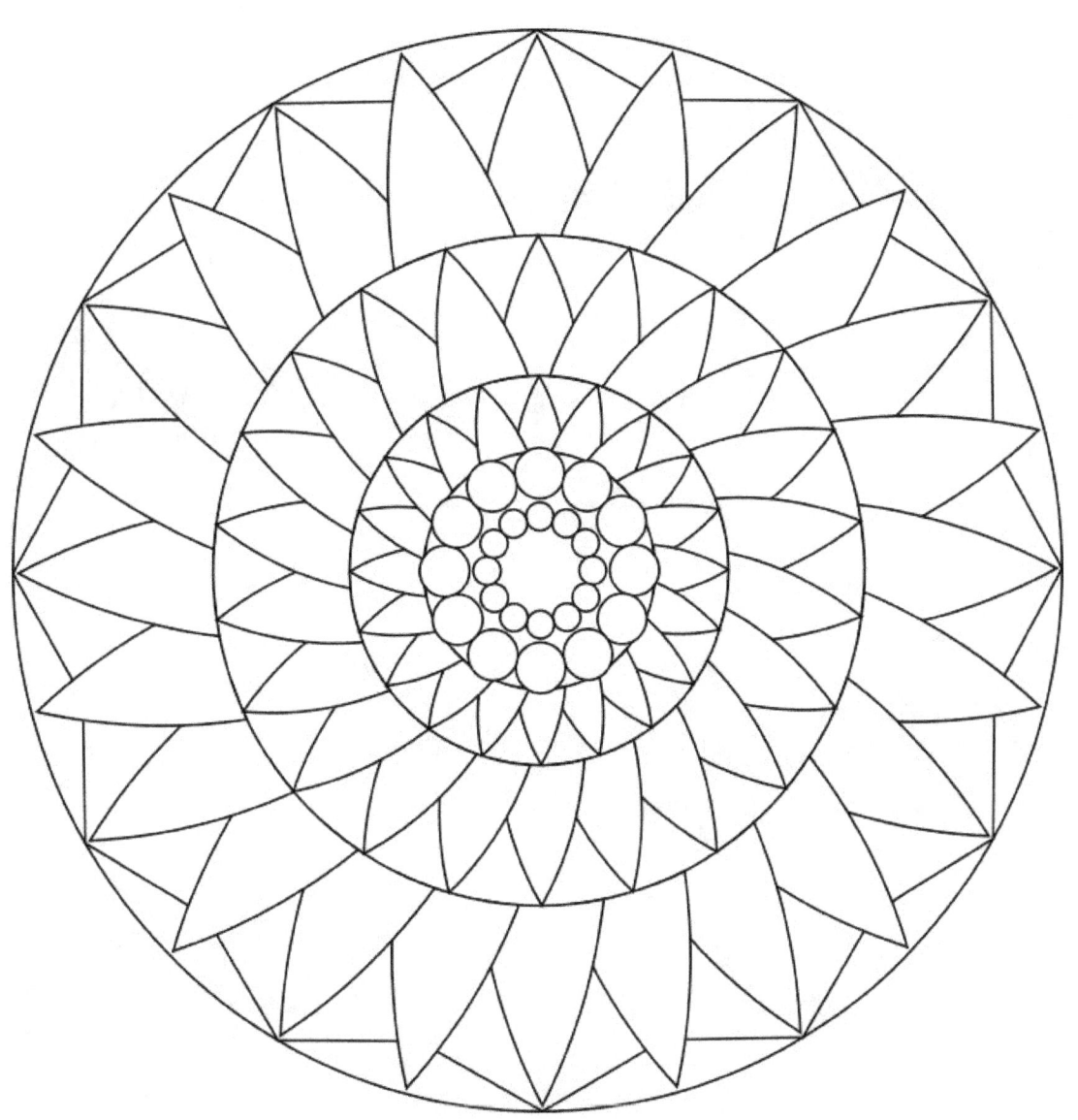

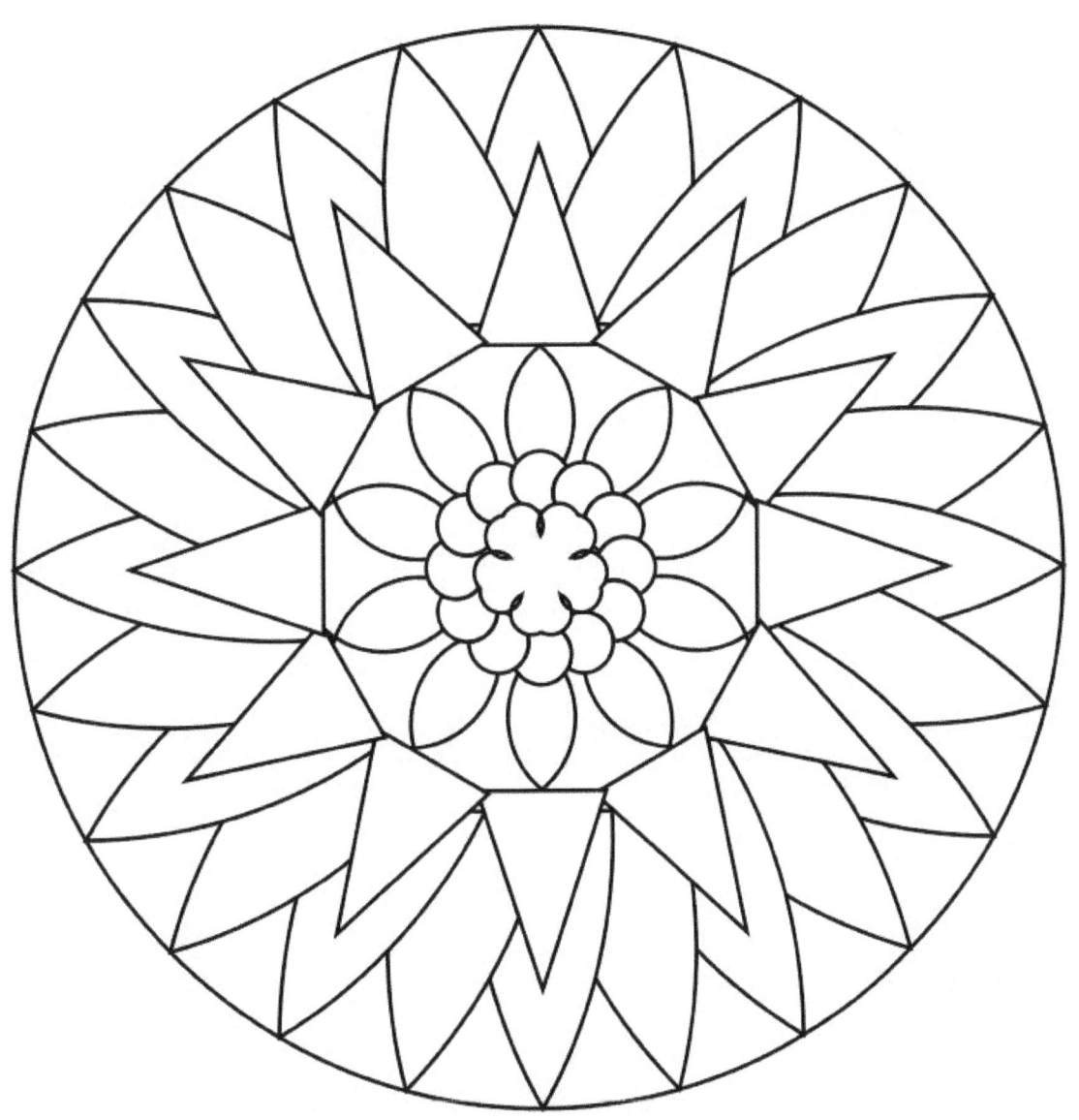

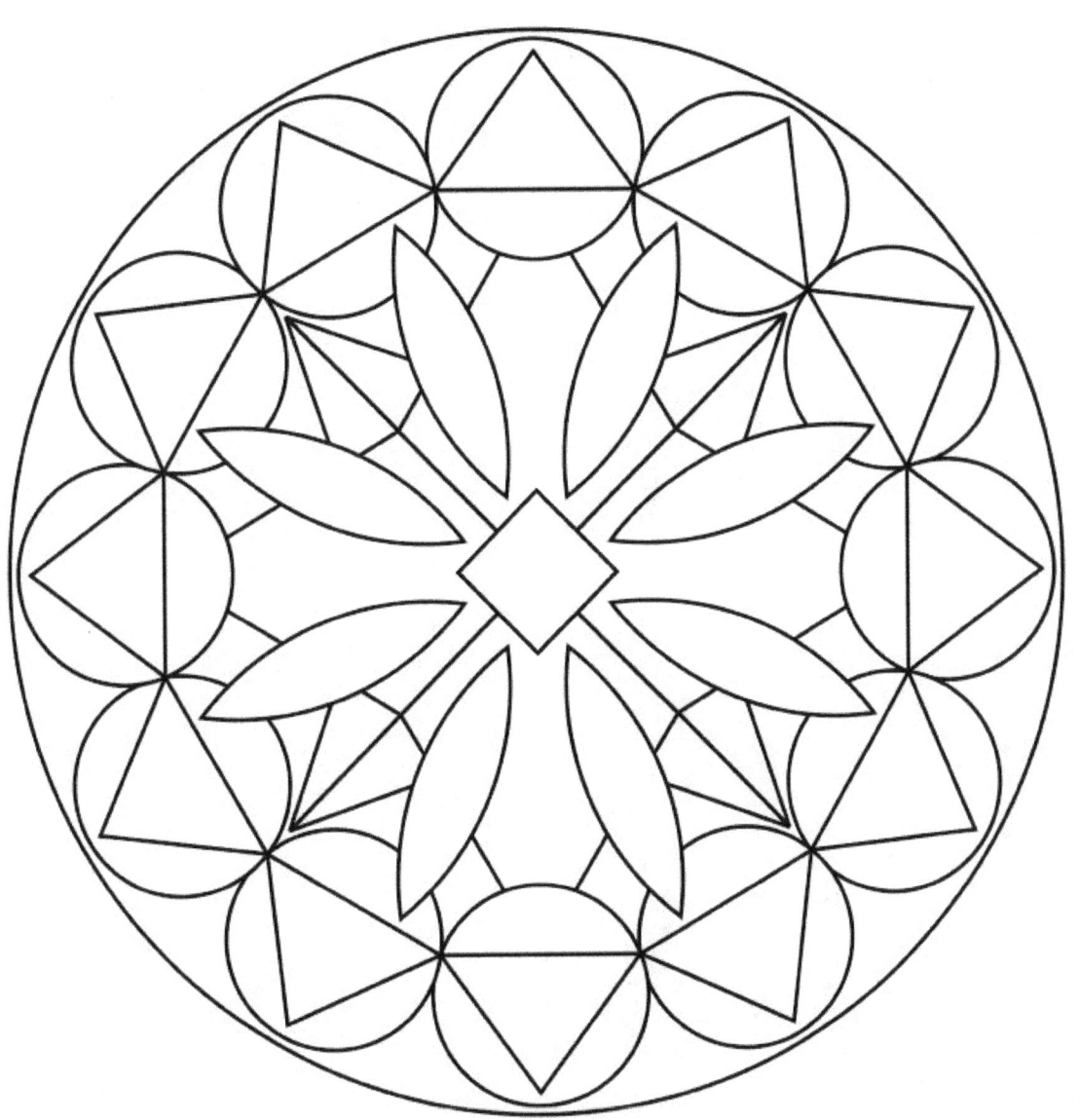

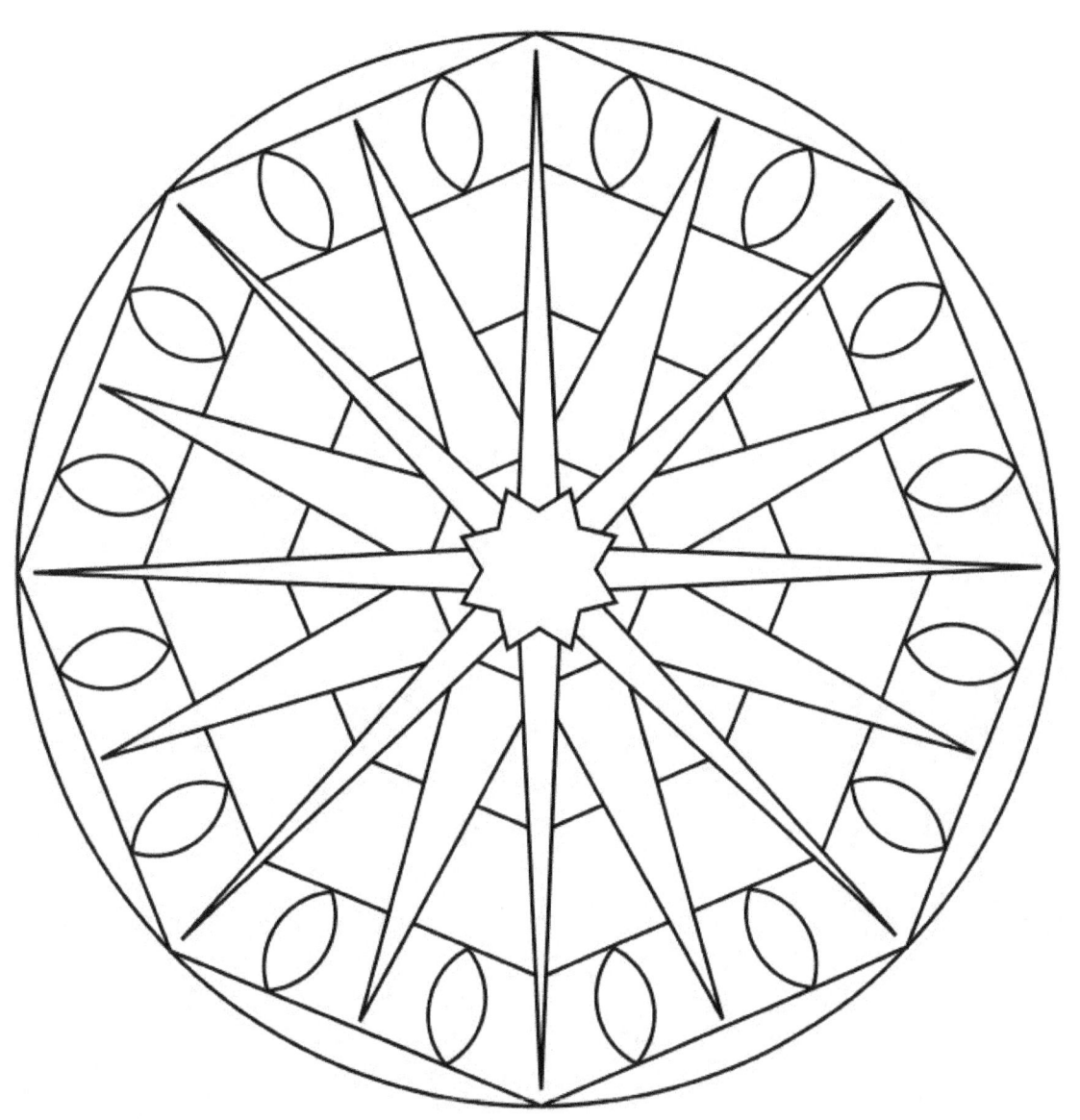

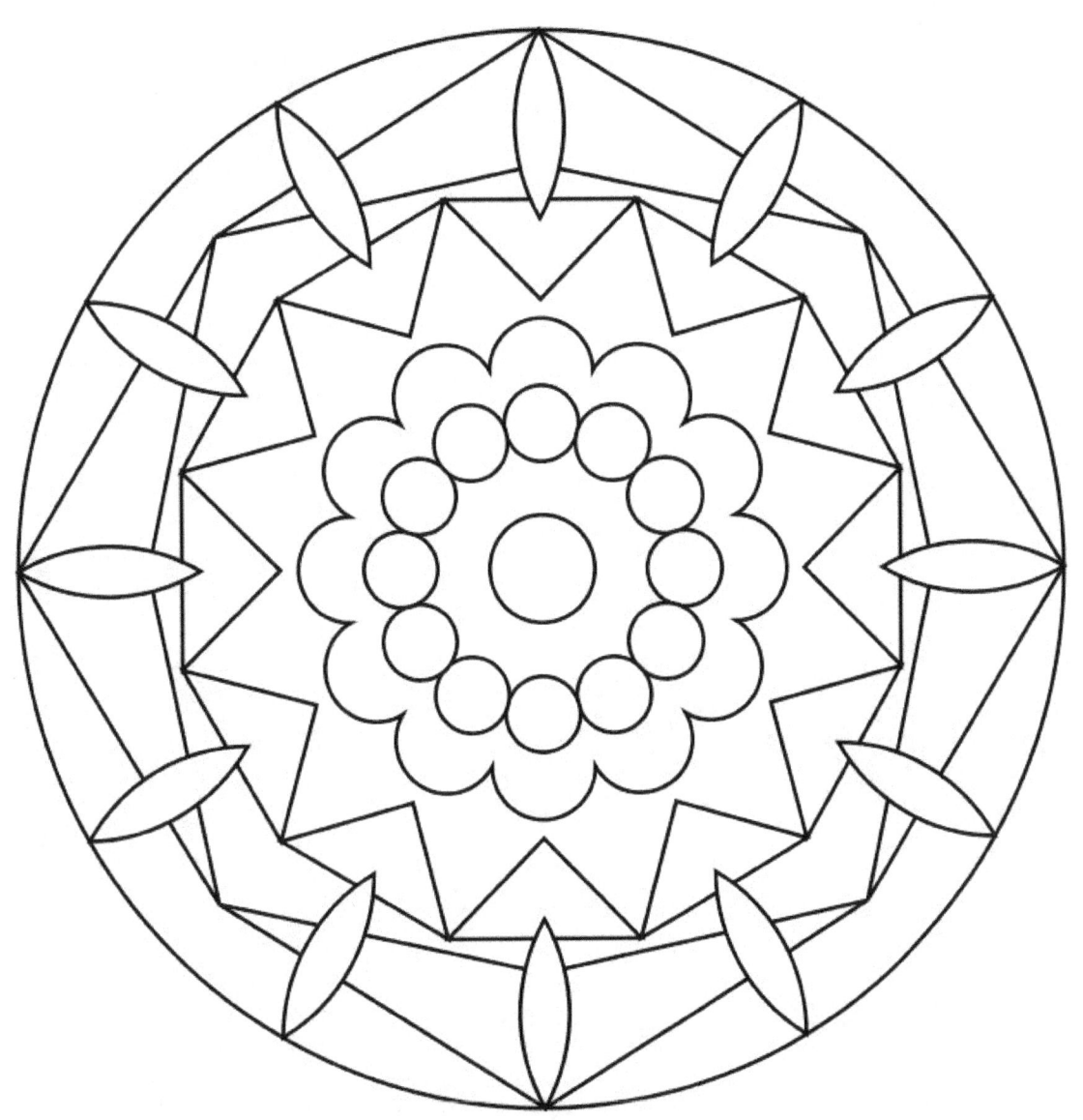

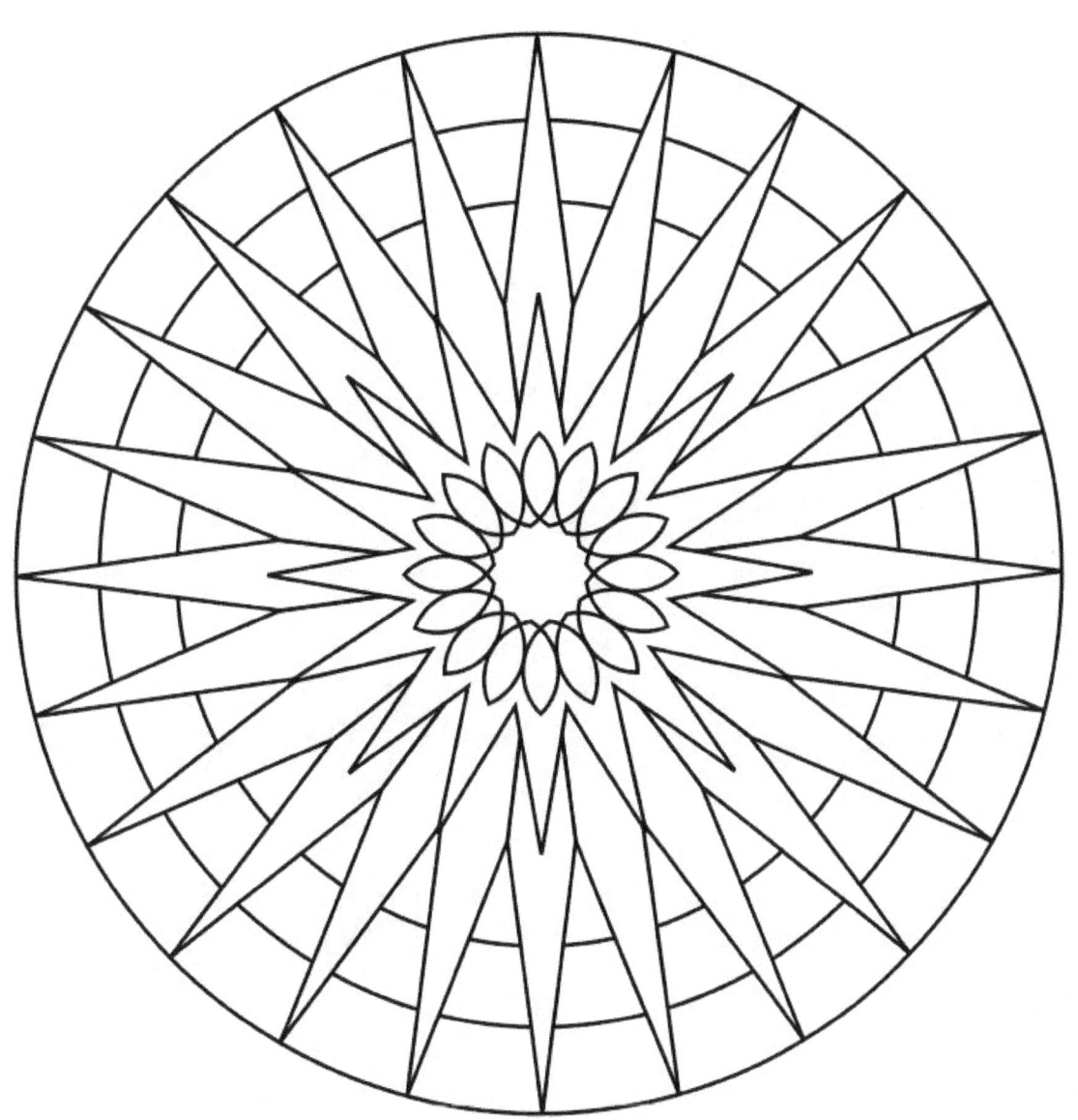

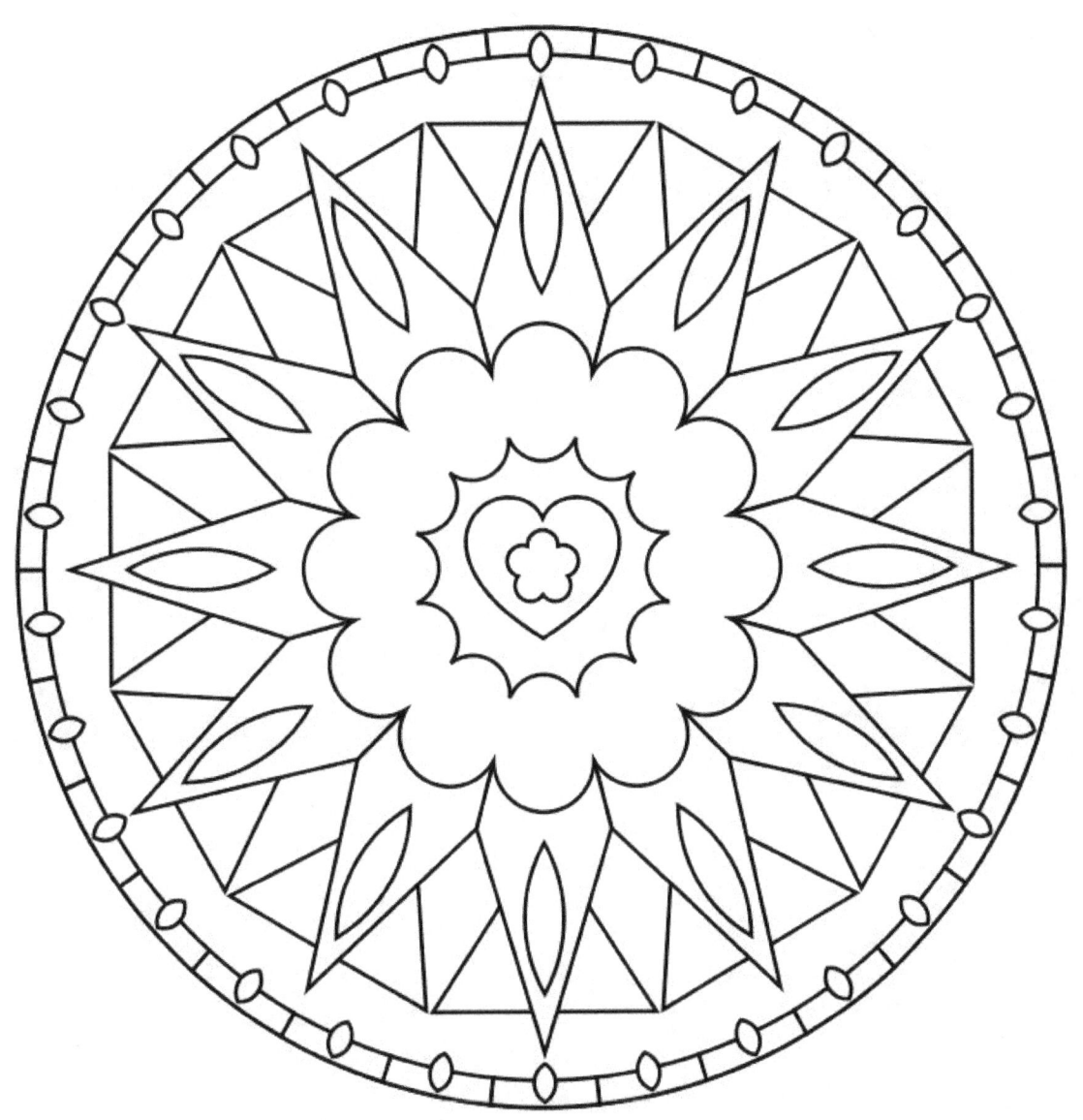

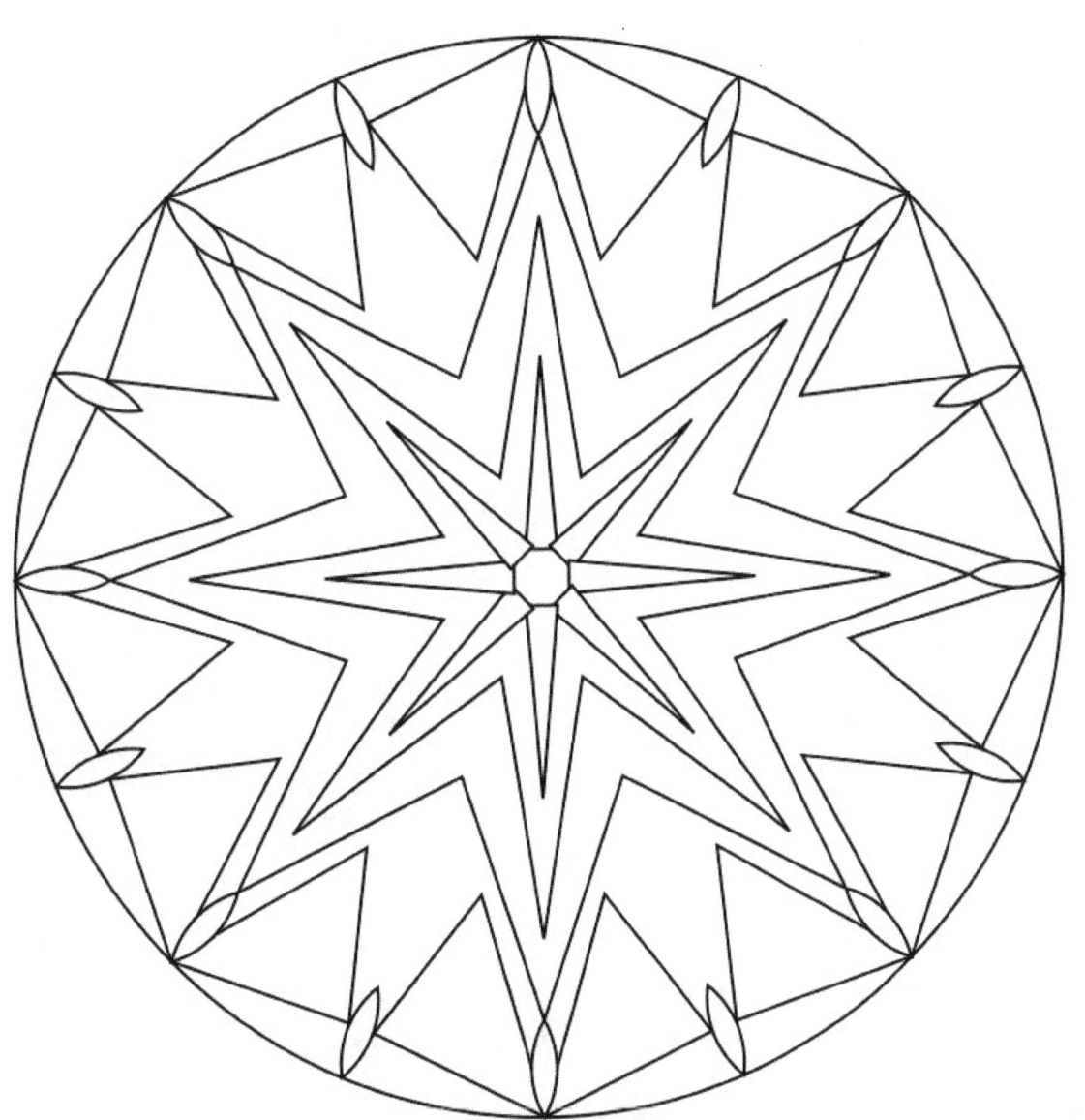

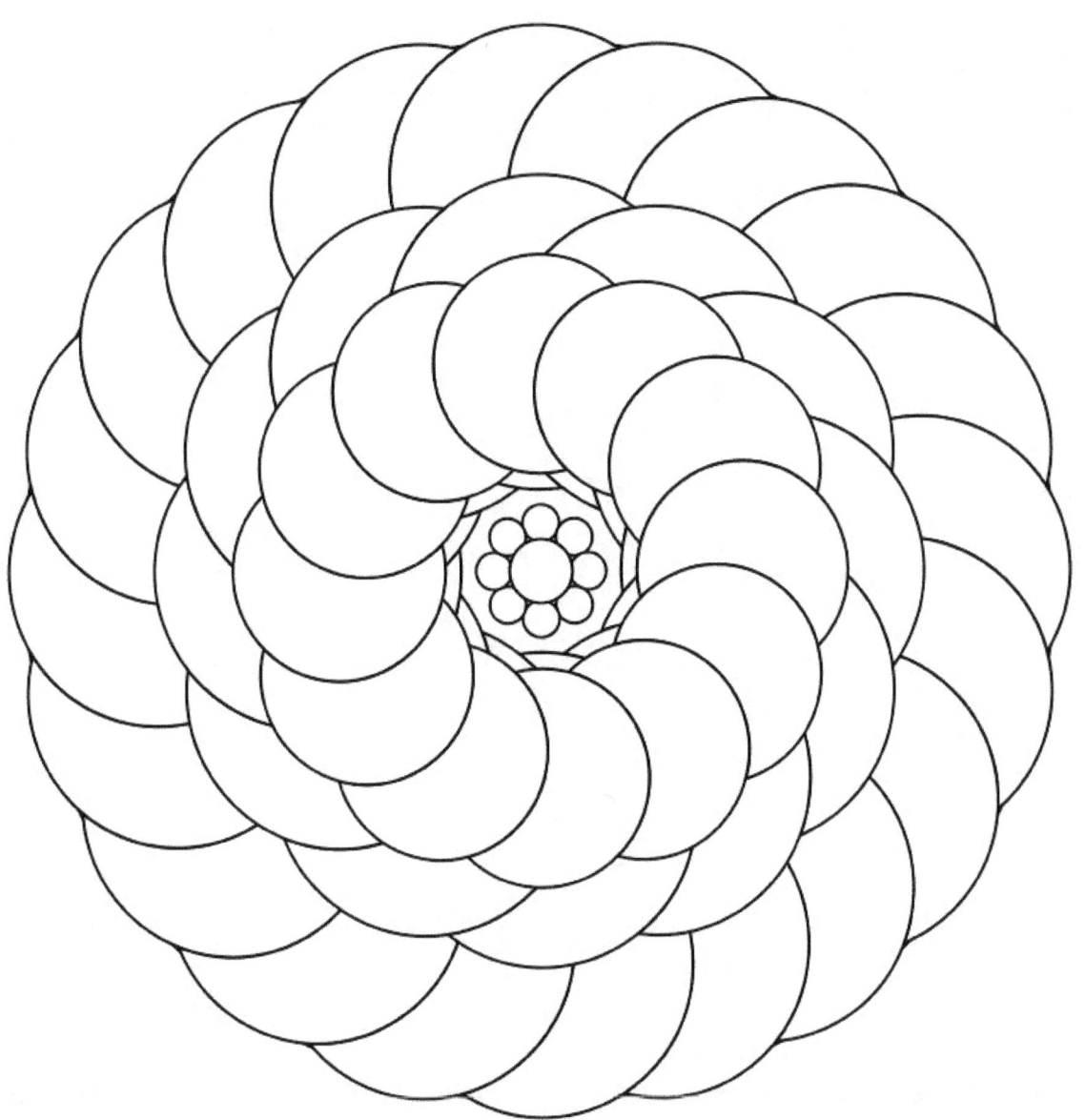

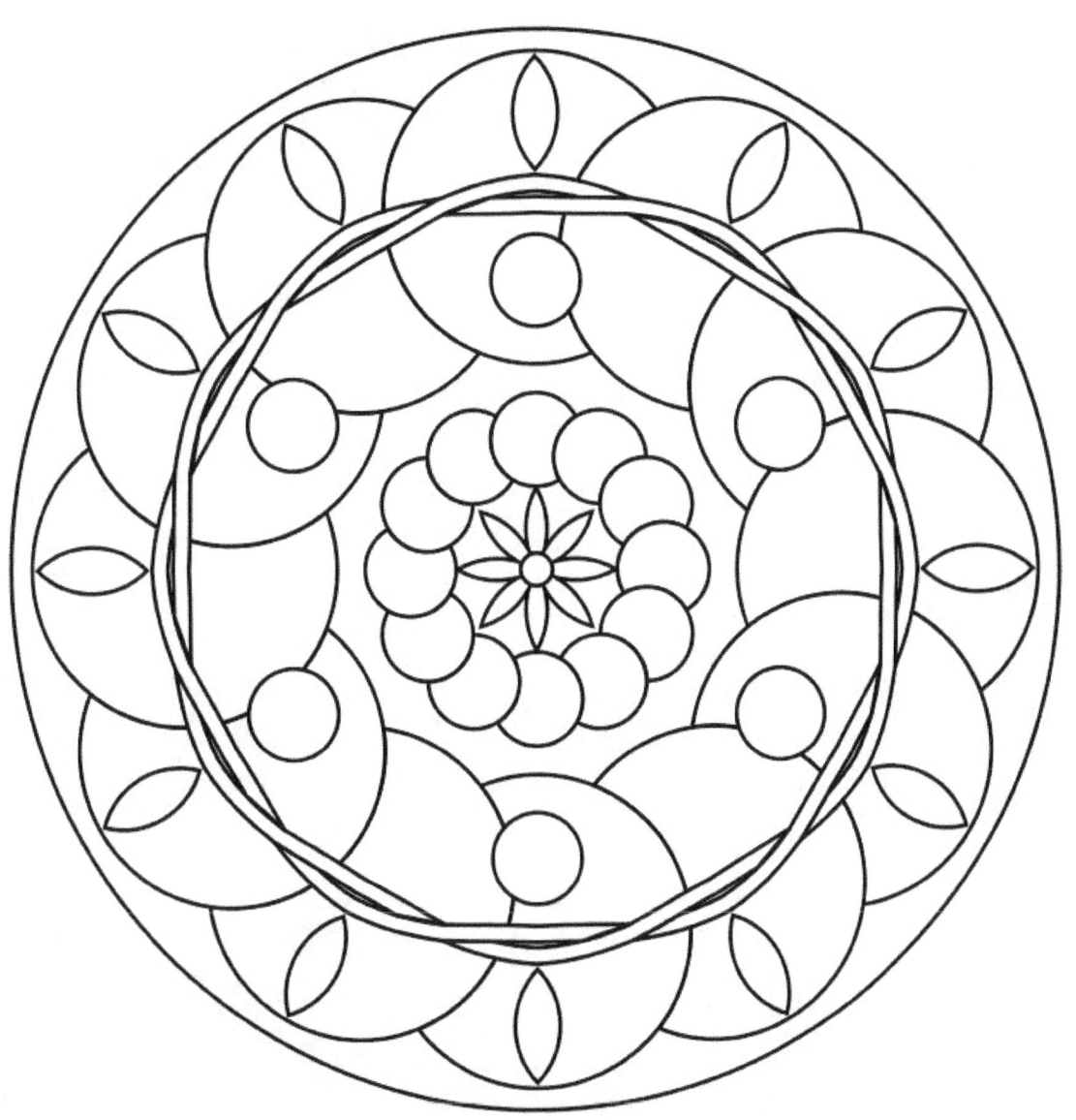

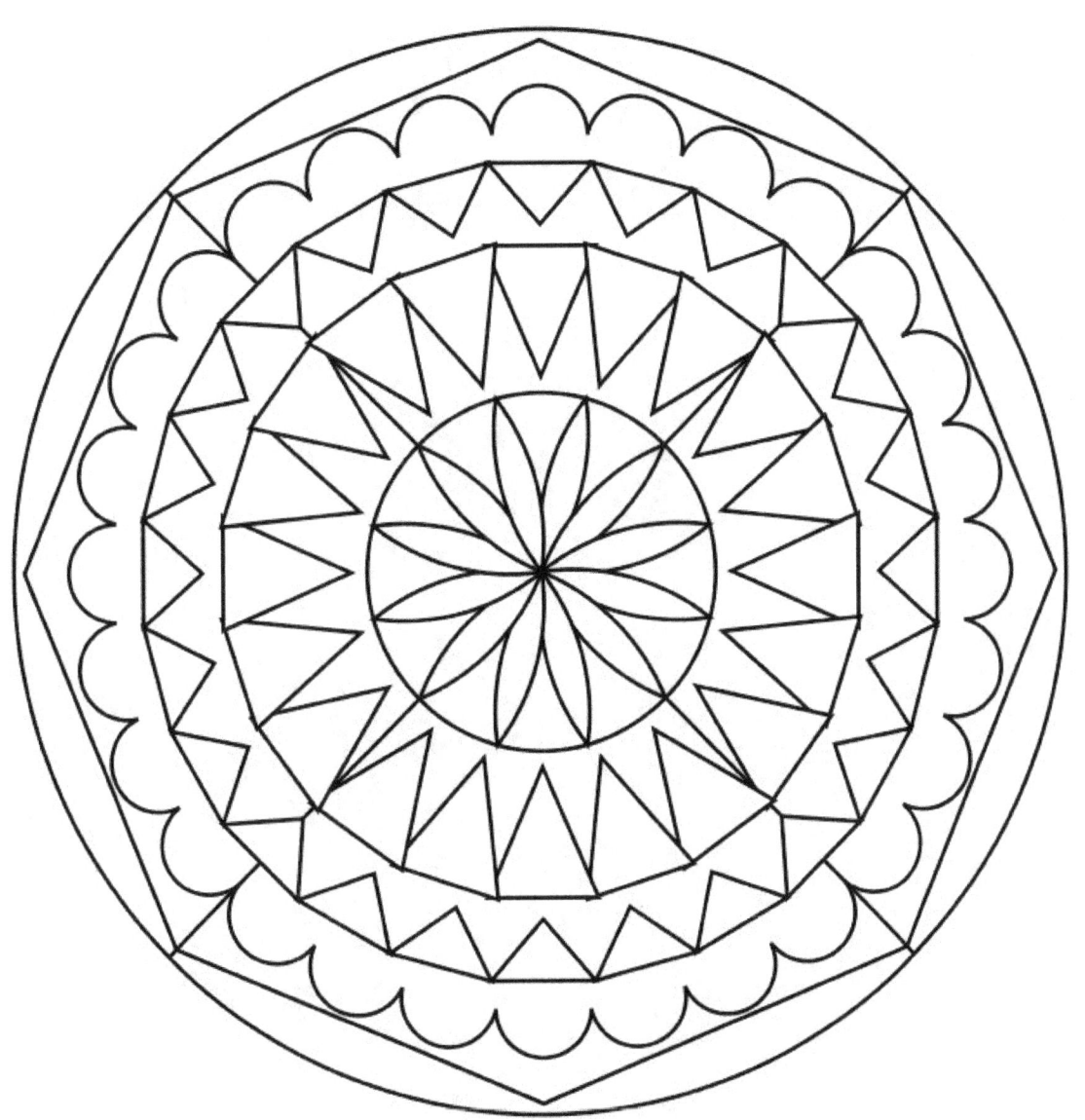

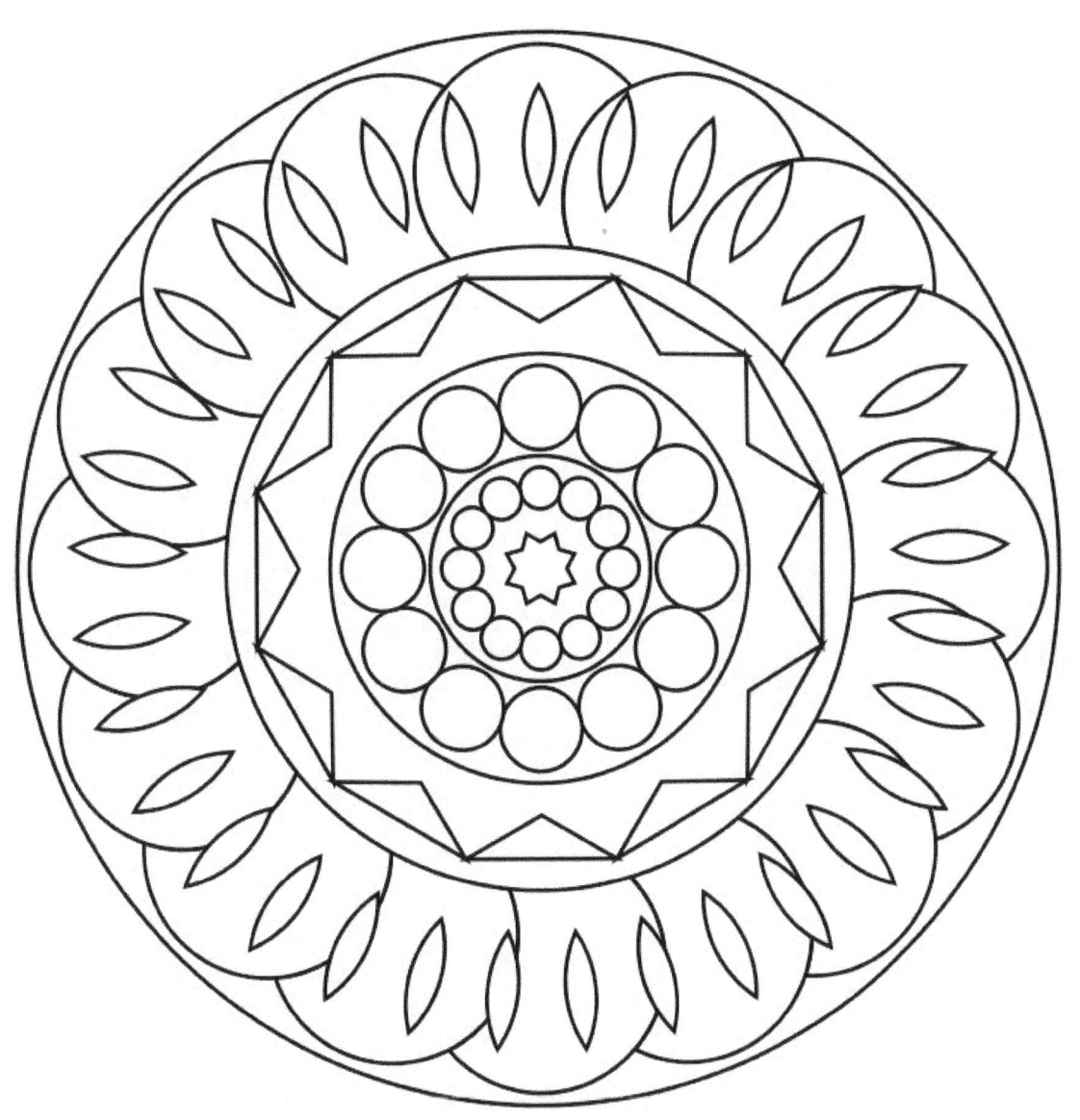

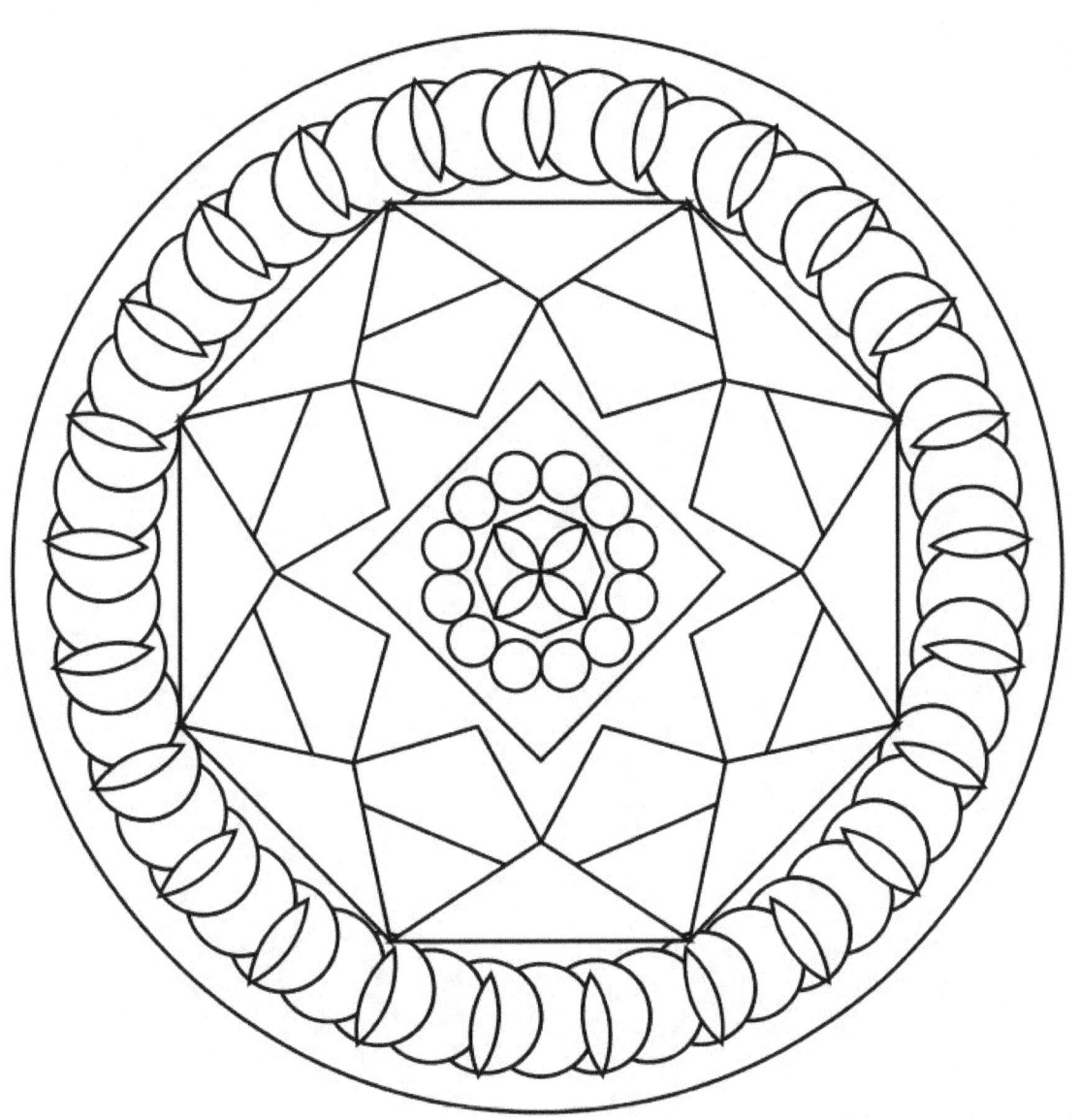

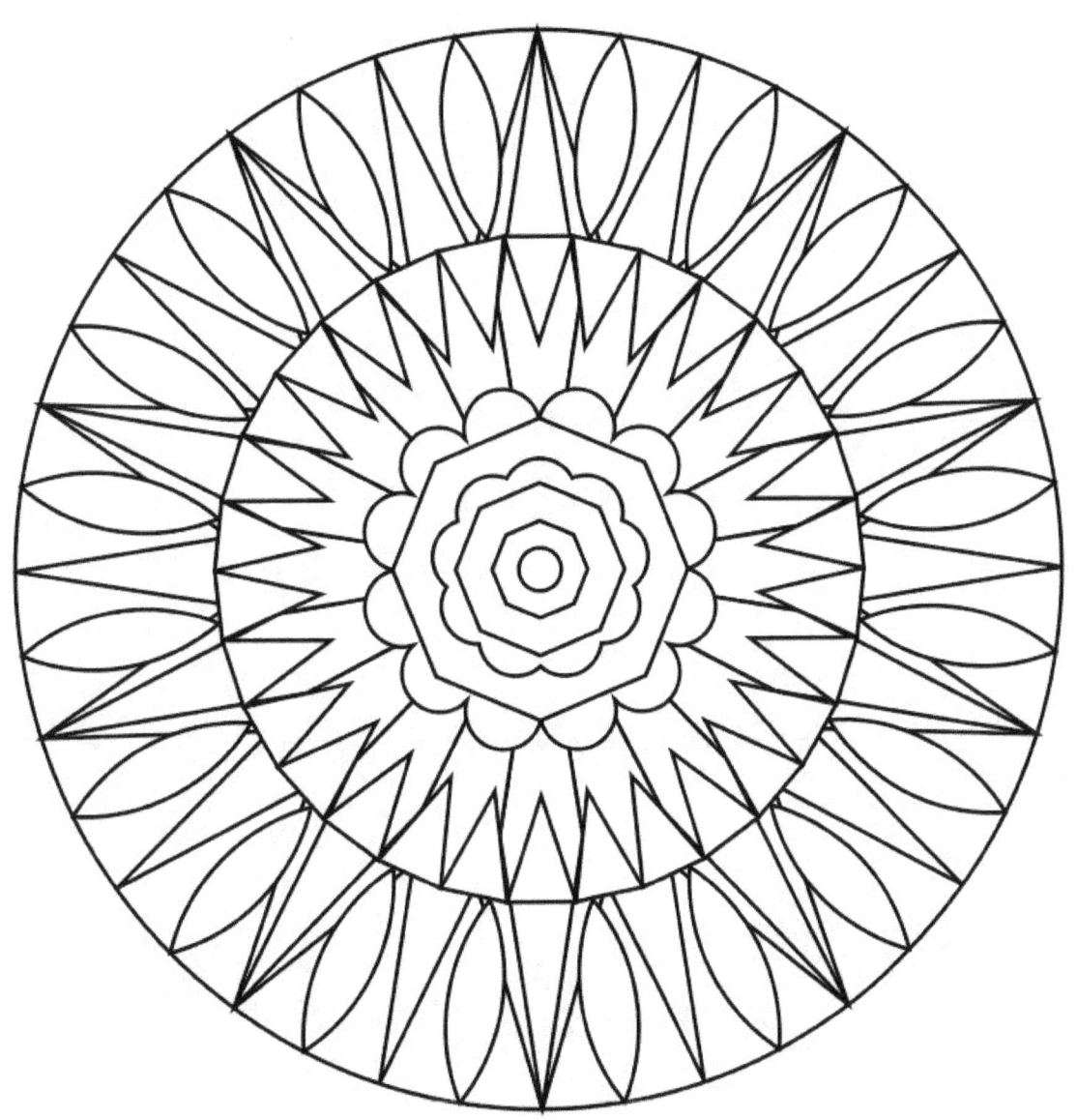

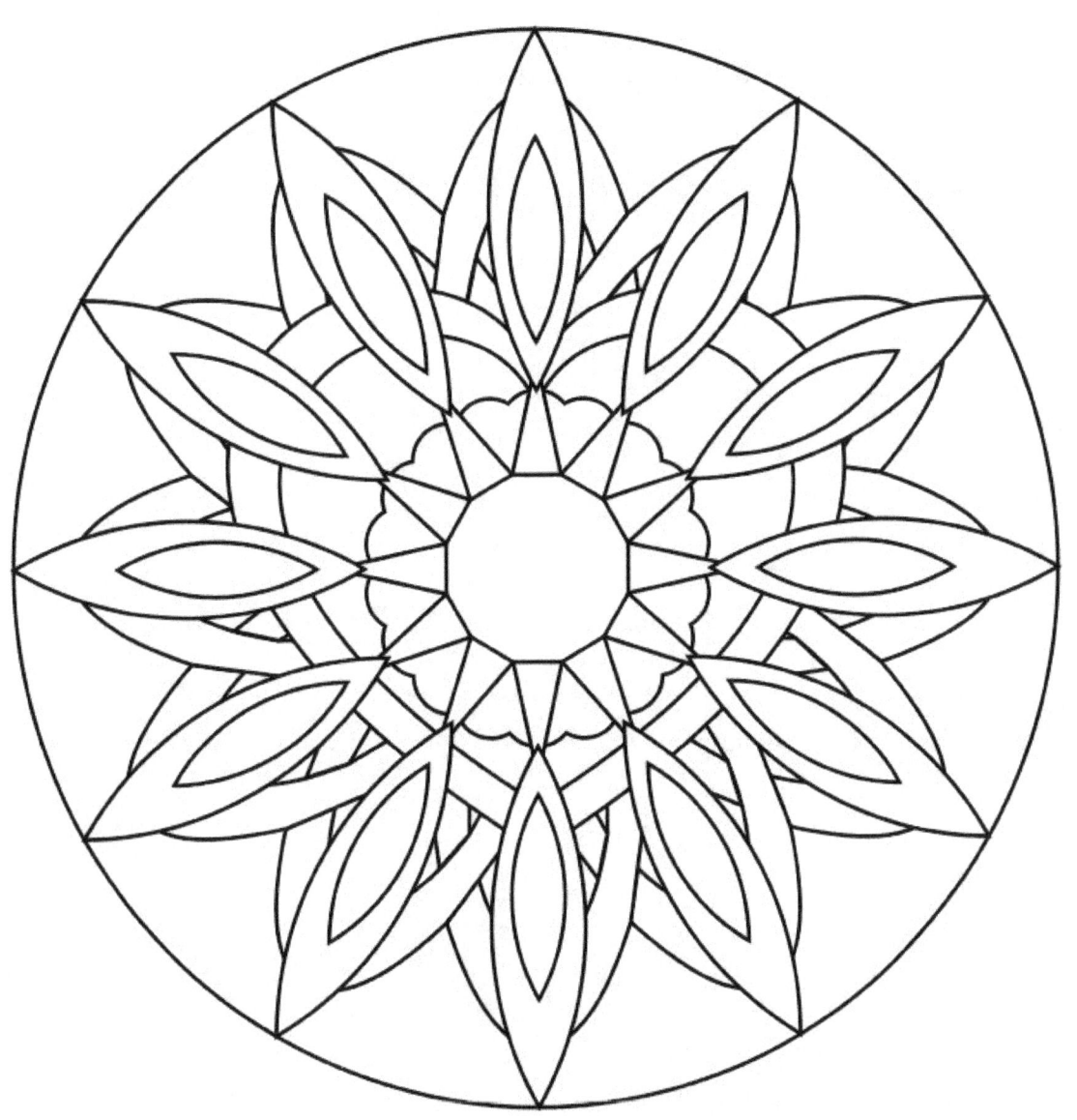

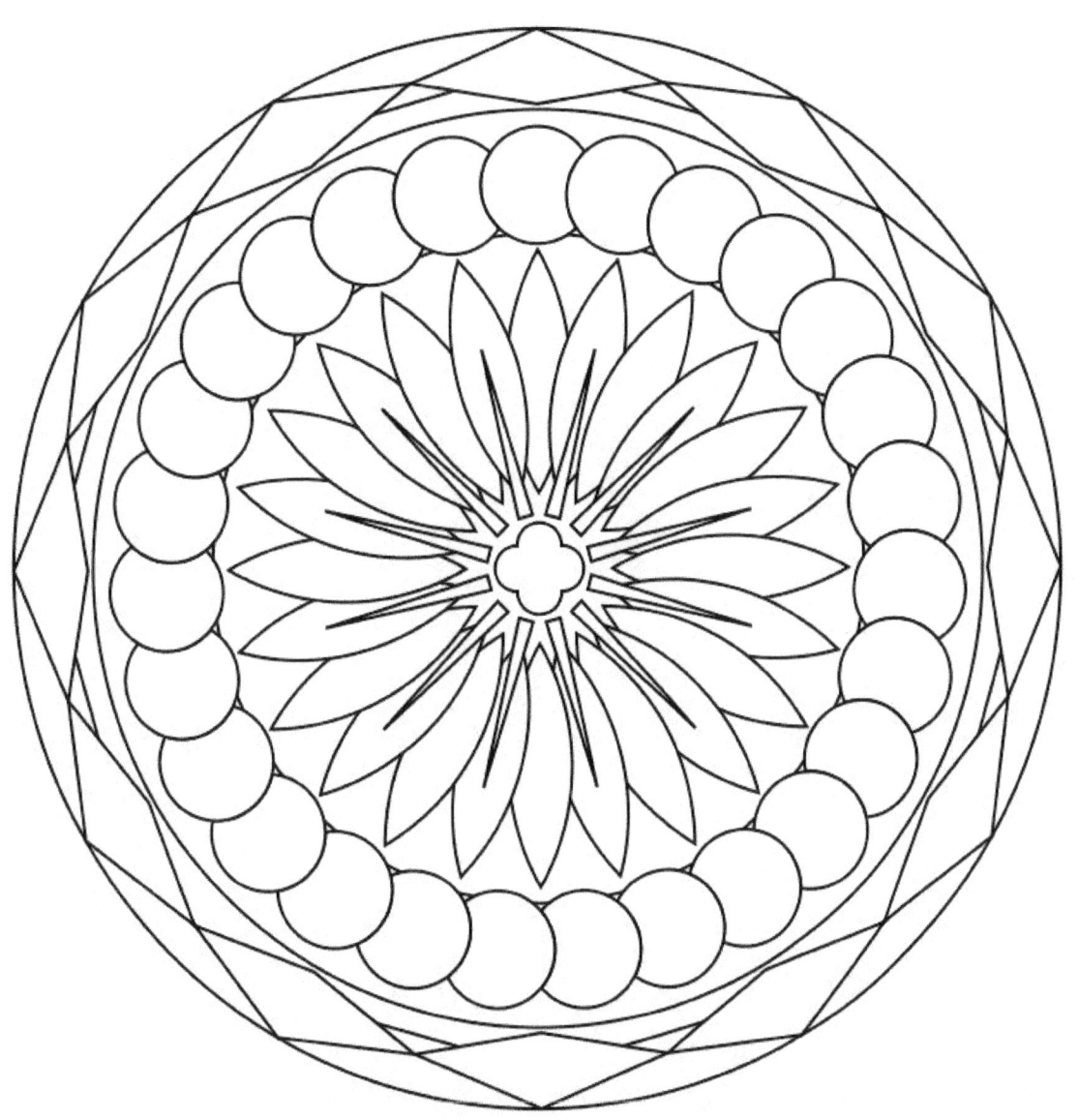

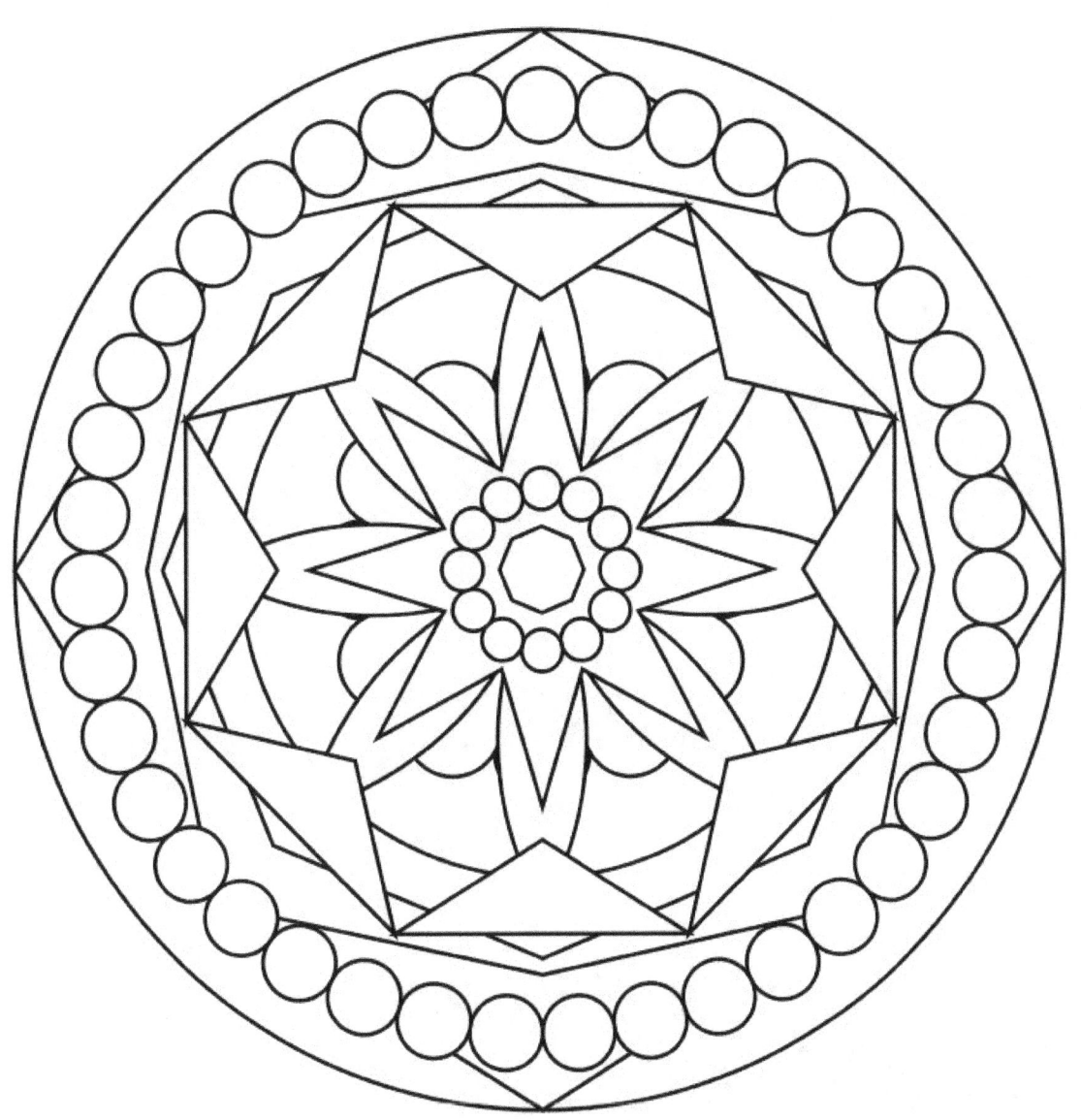

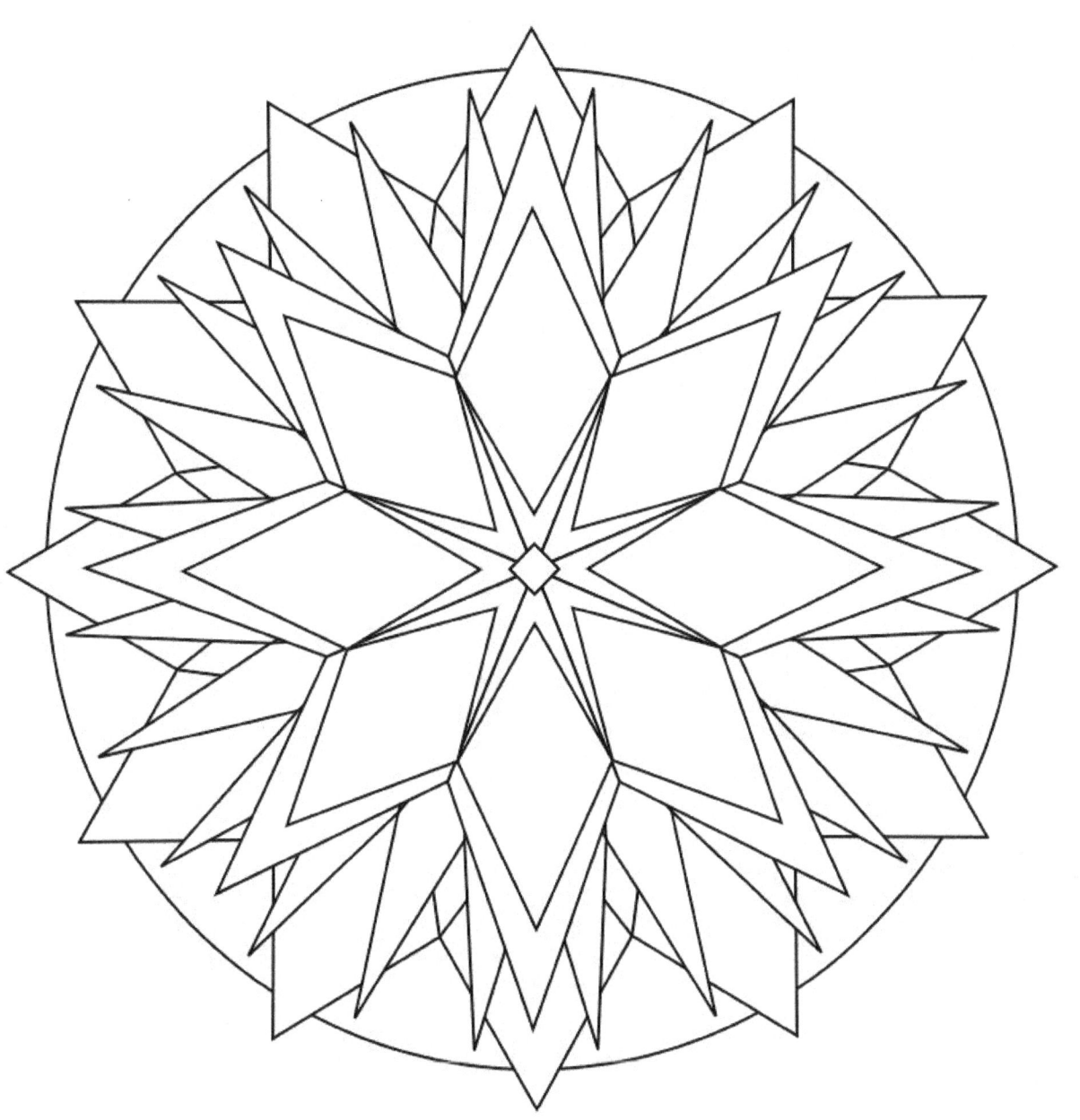

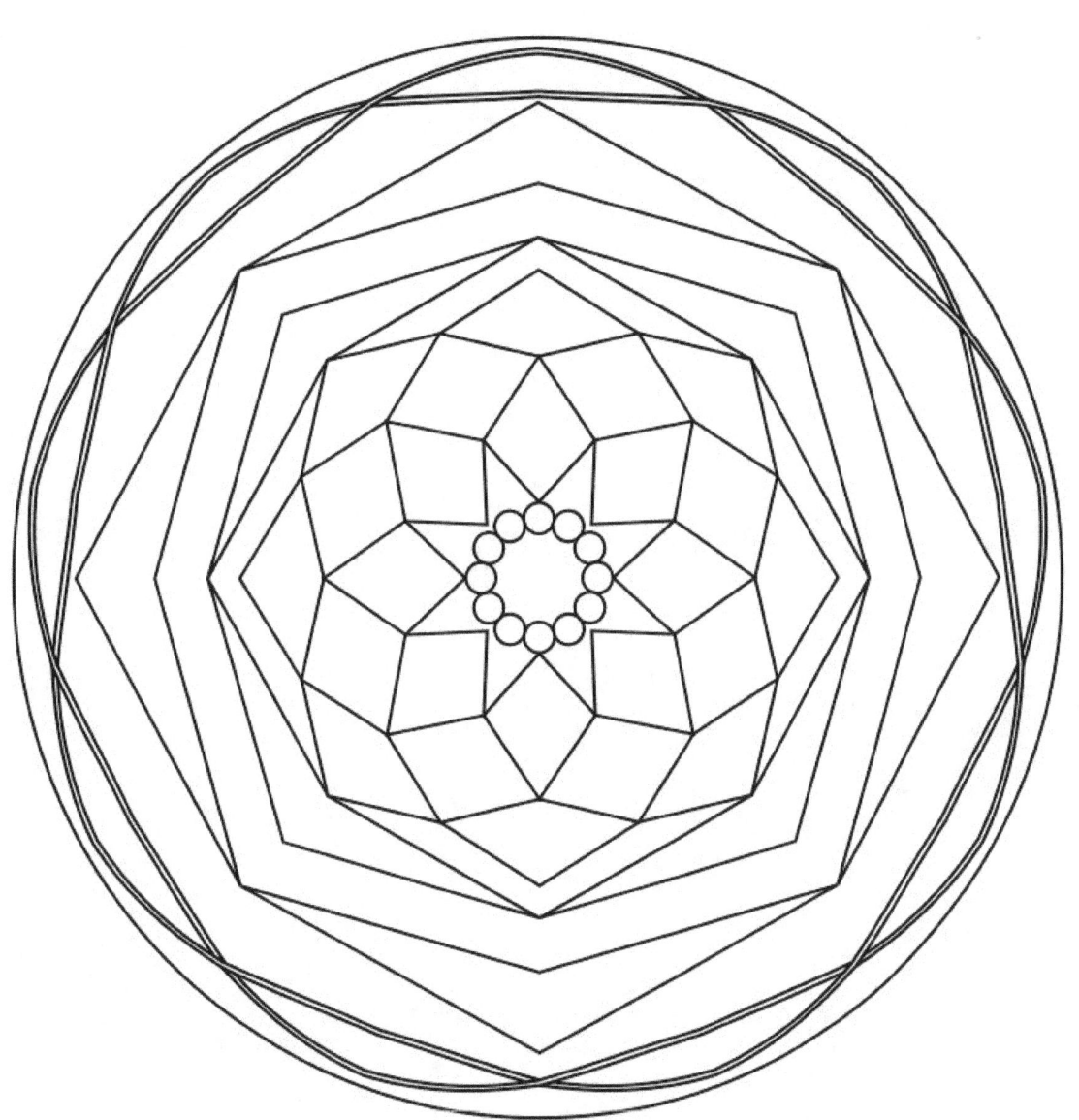

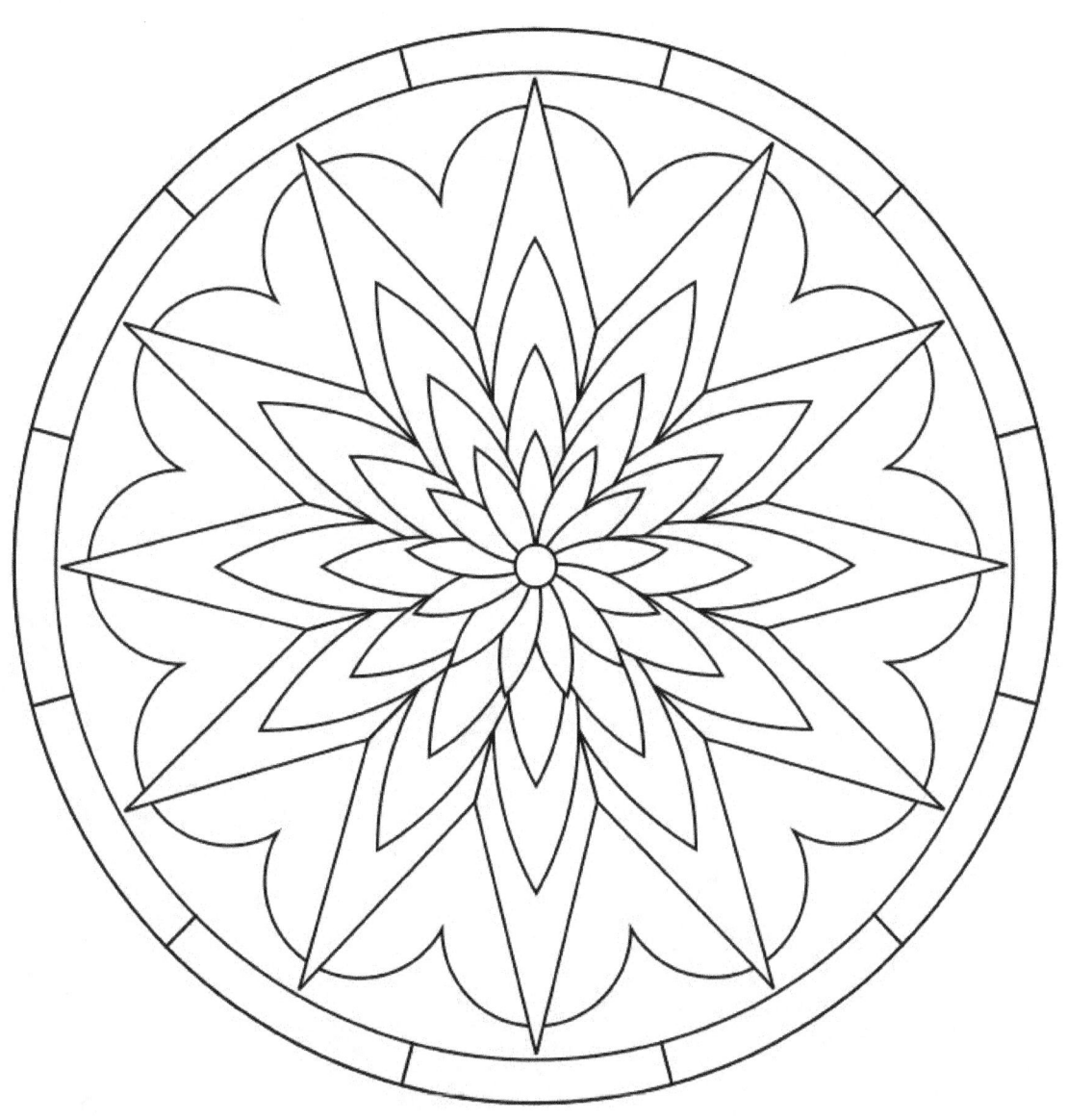

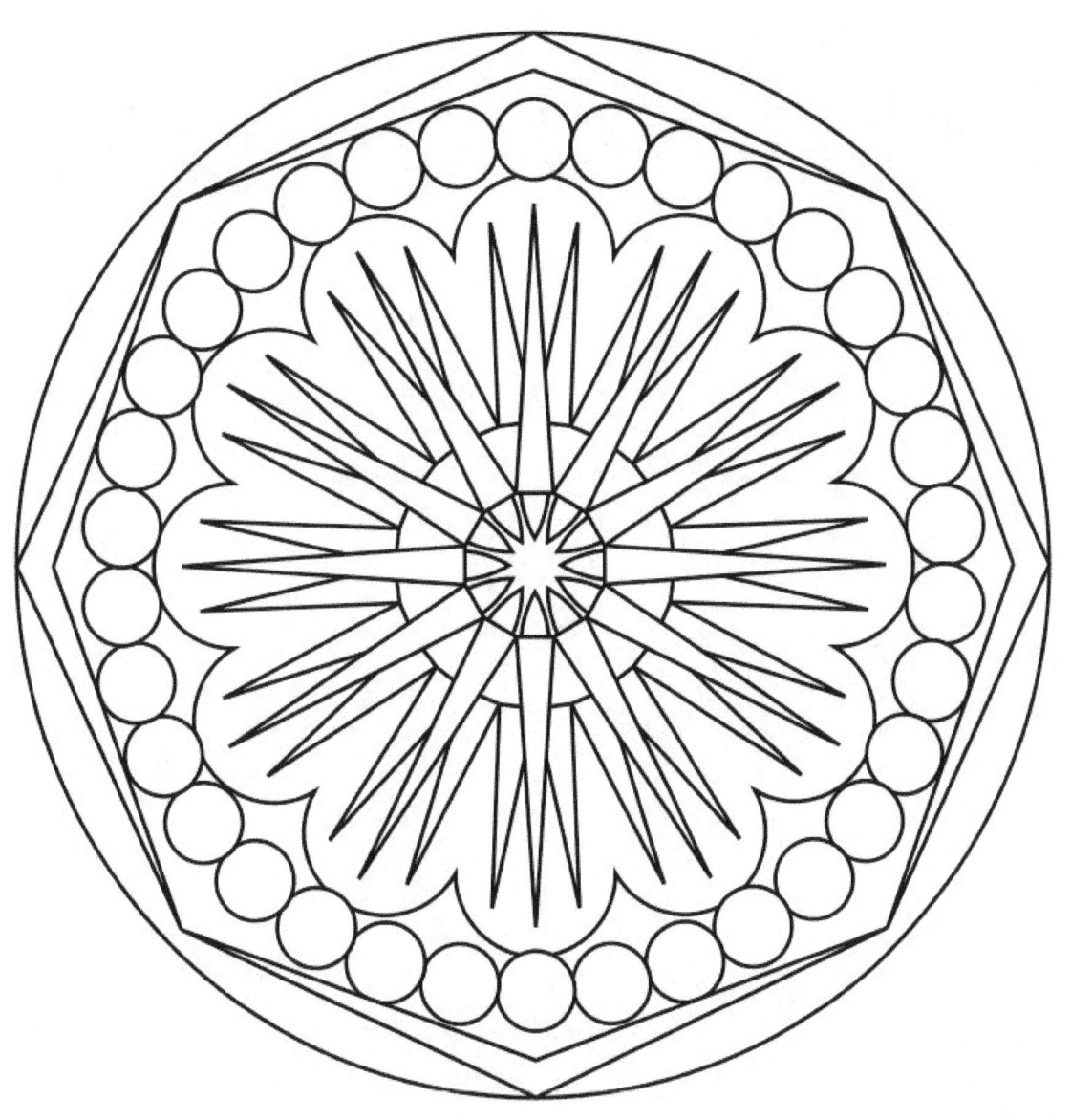

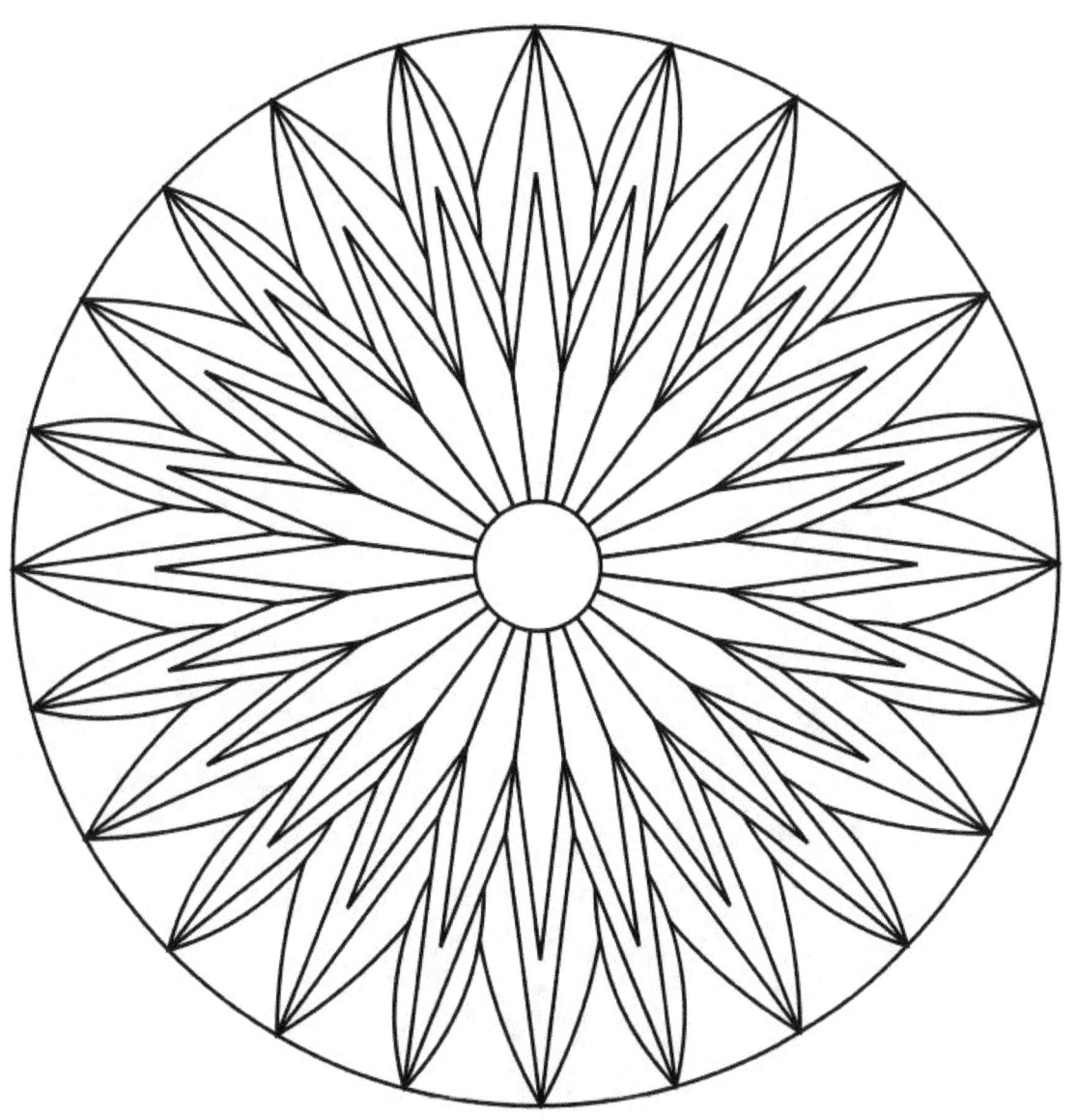

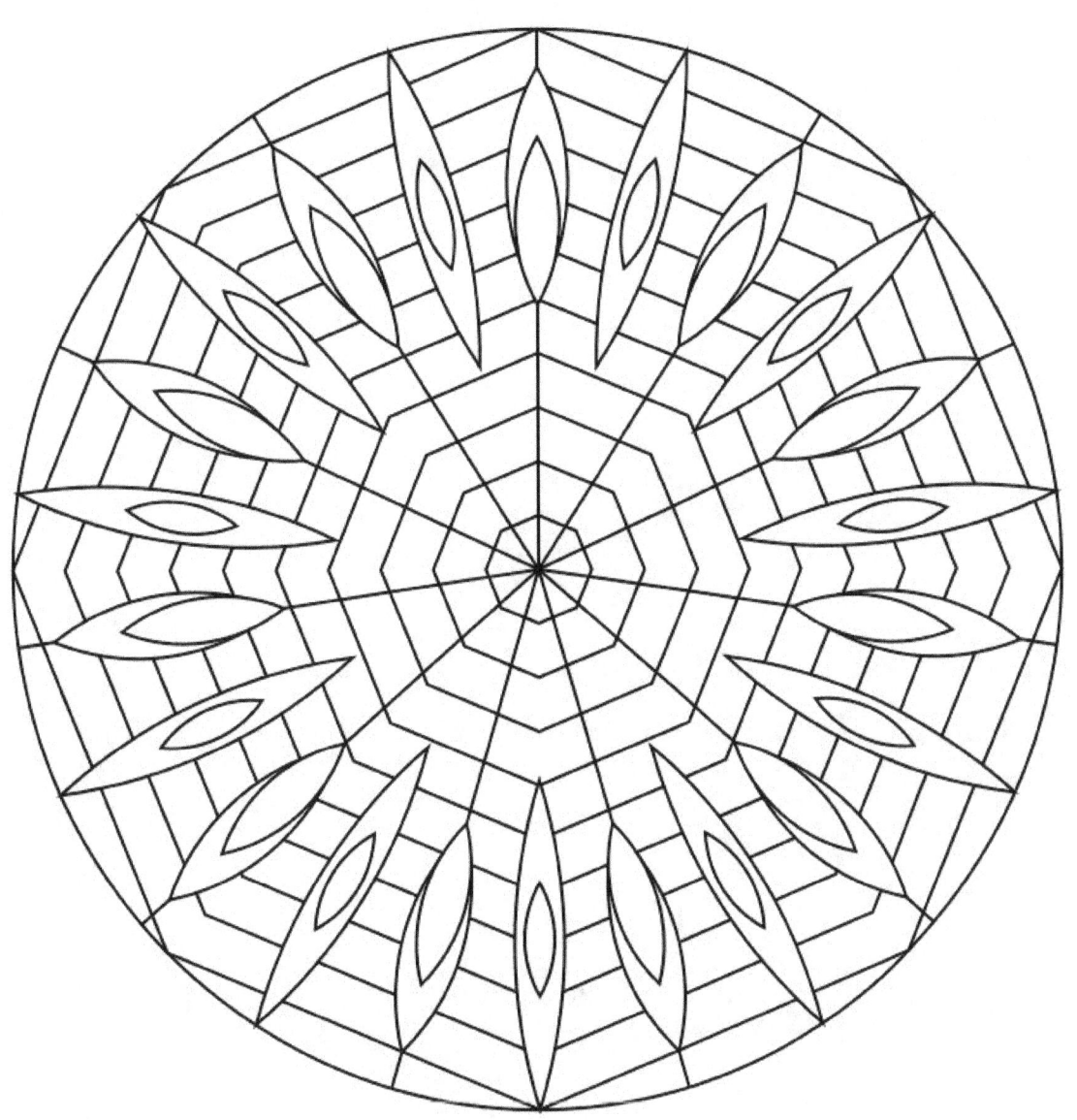

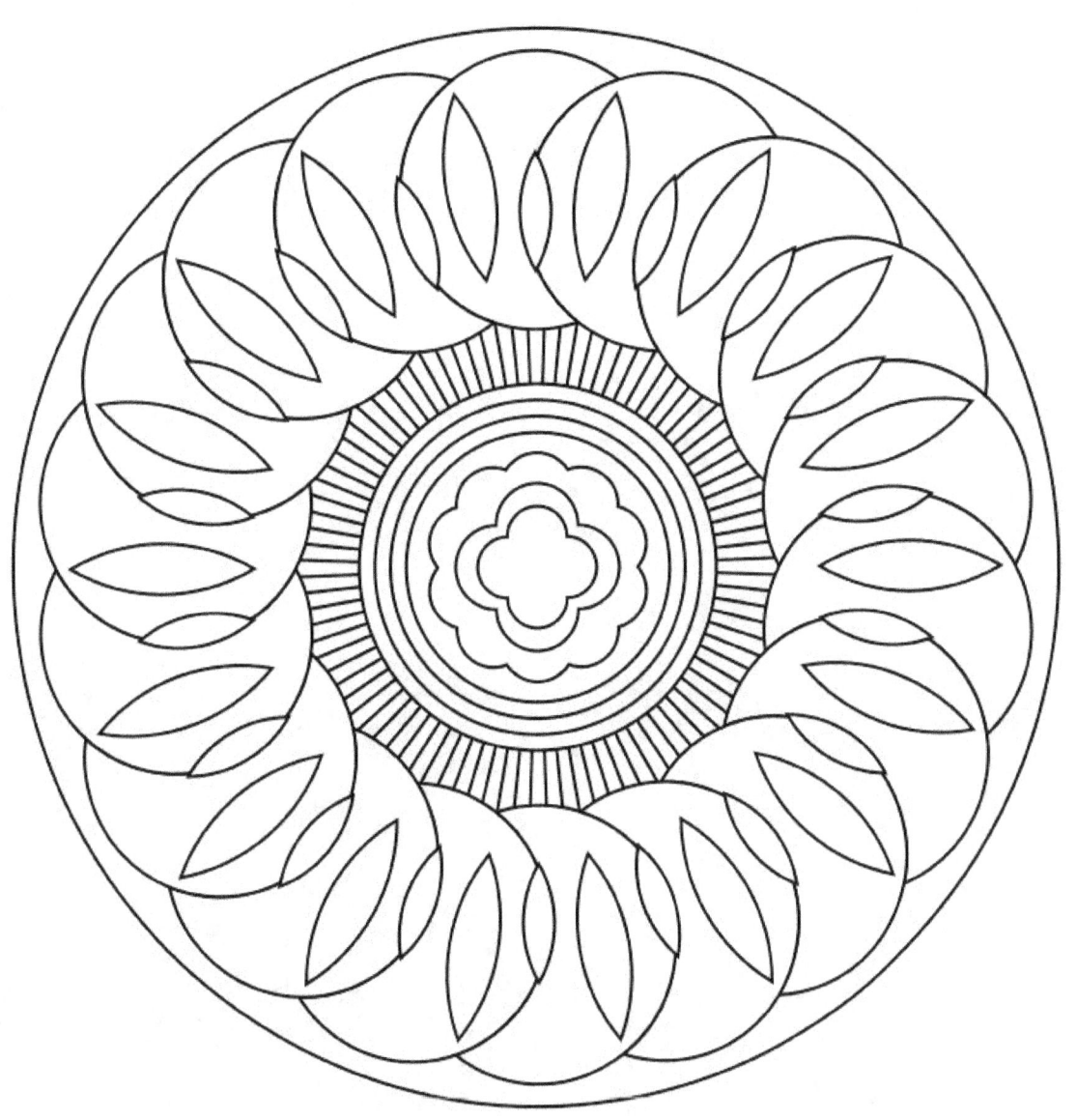

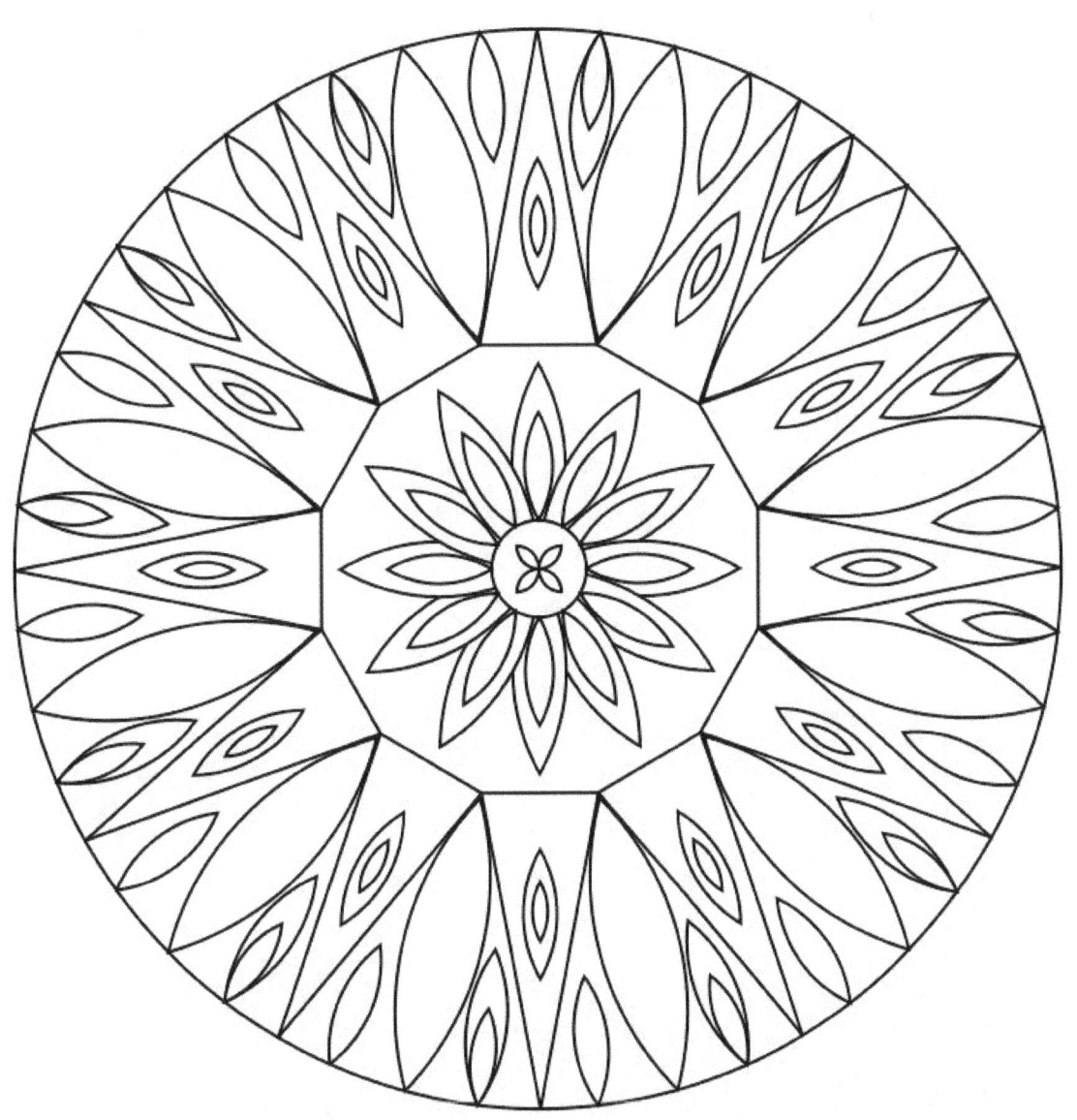

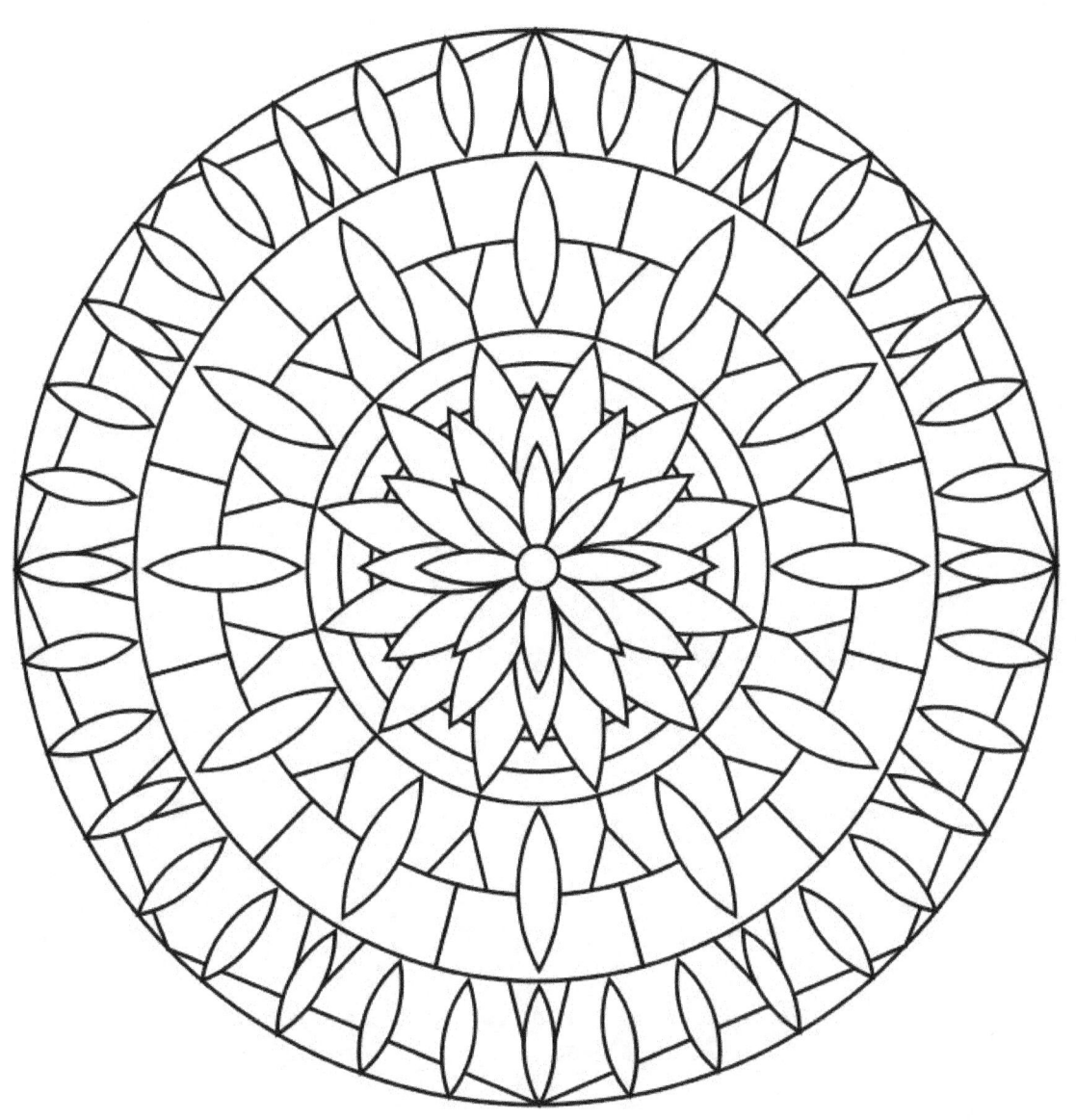

www.ingramcontent.com/pod-product-compliance
Lightning Source LLC
Chambersburg PA
CBHW080822170526
45158CB00009B/2498